Bruce Mazlish is Professor of History at the Massachusetts Institute of Technology. He is a Fellow of the American Academy of Arts and Sciences and sits on the editorial board of such journals as *The Journal of Interdisciplinary History* and *Political Psychology*. His previous books include *Kissinger: The European Mind in American Policy; The Revolutionary Ascetic; James and John Stuart Mill; The Riddle of History;* and *The Western Intellectual History* (with J. Bronowski).

THE MEANING OF
KARL MARX

. . . And, as in private life one differentiates between what a man thinks and says of himself and what he really is and does, so in historical struggles one must differentiate still more the phrases and fancies of parties from their real organism and their real interests, their conceptions of themselves from their reality.—Karl Marx, "Eighteenth Brumaire of Louis Bonaparte" (1852)

THE MEANING OF
KARL MARX

Bruce Mazlish

New York   Oxford
OXFORD UNIVERSITY PRESS
1984

Copyright © 1984 by Bruce Mazlish

Library of Congress Cataloging in Publication Data
Mazlish, Bruce, 1923–
The meaning of Karl Marx.

Bibliography: p.
Includes index.
1. Marx, Karl, 1818–1883.   I. Title.
HX39.5.M395   1984   335.4'092'4   84-9723
ISBN 0-19-503466-X

Printing (last digit):   9 8 7 6 5 4 3 2 1

Printed in the United States of America

To JM, TM, and NG

Acknowledgment

I thank colleagues and friends for reading draft chapters, including Bernard Avishai, Harry Lubasz, Robert E. MacMaster, Leo Marx, S. M. Miller, Wolf Shäfer, Tony Smith, Robert C. Tucker, Fred Weinstein, and Robert Paul Wolff. At least one or more suffered a mild form of apoplexy over one or more positions I was taking, but were reasonably polite in their murmurs of dissatisfaction; clearly, they are not to be held responsible for any faults in the book, and, just as clearly, I benefited from their comments.

John Stachel, Willis H. Truitt, and Mark Wartofsky kindly responded to my requests for draft copies of their articles in progress on various facets of Marx and Marxism, and I thank them. Norman Levine invited me to present a draft of Chapter I at a conference at the University of Maryland, "Marxism: One Hundred Years Later" (April 16, 1983), and has taken a warm interest in its publication. My friend Ralph Buultjens arranged a lecture and debate between us on Marx, at the New School for Social Research (April 28, 1983), which gave me a chance to advance some of my interpretations in public, and I wish to record my appreciation.

Sheldon Meyer, my editor at Oxford University Press, made all the right suggestions, and then exercised just the right amount of restraint in letting me work them out in my own way. Pamela Nicely, assistant editor at Oxford, deftly copyedited the manuscript, and I much appreciate her careful assistance.

Melinda Gliddens at M.I.T. deserves special thanks. She took numerous versions of my squiggly, handwritten drafts and produced readable chapters on the word processor, accompanying their return to me with useful comments. The versions that unrolled from the computer printer gave at least the appearance of clarity, and encouraged me to go on.

Neva Goodwin read and reread the entire manuscript. Her editorial improvements, stylistic and substantive, are everywhere. I have literally "talked out" the book to her, with a resulting dialogue that makes the book spiritually as much hers as mine.

Anthony and Jared Mazlish, my sons, wondered why I was bothering to write a book on Marx; I hope that now they will understand, and even read it with a measure of approval.

Cambridge, Mass., Bruce Mazlish
February 1984

Contents

THE MEANING OF
KARL MARX

Introduction

Although this book is, on one level, a life and work of Karl Marx, it is not simply a biography. There are a number of excellent biographies already existent, and I do not wish to add another. Rather, I have attempted a close textual analysis of both the life and the work, using each to illuminate the other. I have not felt obliged to give every detail of Marx's life, though I hope my account includes the main ones, nor to deal critically with every letter, tract, and book he wrote. (In the Notes and Bibliography, I have tried to indicate where the interested reader can find further information.)

In reading Marx in this manner, I have tried to follow his line of thought, its leaps and tergivisations, rather than extracting, or imposing, a clear, logical exposition where it is lacking in the original. I want to follow the actual movement of his thought, which is often erratic, and to share it with the reader.

I have concentrated on trying to understand Marx's real meaning, and to do so in a combined empathic and critical spirit. Meaning, however, is a matter of context. If I say, for example, "The house blue it," you will recognize immediately that the sentence is syntactically silly. If I then say, "No, I meant the house blew it," you will accept it gramatically, but wonder what possible meaning the sentence could have. Only if I can supply you with a contextual framework—for example, that a casino's scheme for beating a gambler's system has misfired—will the sentence take on meaning.[1] So, too, Marx's texts—his sentences—acquire their meaning, for him and for us, only when we are acquainted with the world that serves as context for what he writes. That world is both his personal and public sphere in the 19th century, as well as the world that comes after him, and supplies a context, in turn, for our understanding of what he is saying to us, i.e., what he means.

Marxist studies are almost always controversial. While I have attempted to be non-polemical in tone and spirit, and to avoid engaging in "theological" controversies as such, I make no pretense to be neutral on the matters so vehemently dealt with by Marx himself. My title, in fact, is slightly misleading. There is no single meaning of Marx—*the* Meaning—and no final reading of his life and work. My reading, then, is simply a contribution, though I hope an enriching one, to the continuous effort at an understanding of Marx and Marxism.

Such an effort is of great—shall I pun and say critical?—importance. As I contend in the first chapter, Marxism is Marx writ large. As such, it is a secular religion—a term I prefer to ideology—which has spread over large areas of the globe. My initial chapter is simply an attempt to give a context, stressing the industrial revolution, for my treatment of Marx's life and work; it is not a full-scale explanation of how and why Marxism, as a secular religion, arose and spread, i.e., it is not a history of Marxism.

The second chapter is about Marx's poetry; his juvenilia reveal many of his deepest aspirations. In this chapter, I also seek to situate Marx in the romantic movement of his time, especially in its critical approach to capitalist society. Chapter III examines his school leaving essays, one on choosing a career and one on religion; unlike most commentators on Marx, I take seriously the role played by his training in the Christian religion in shaping his thought (while I also try to estimate the significance of his Jewish background). Chapter IV reexamines his relation to his father and family. Chapter V seeks to understand the democratic and dictatorial tensions in Marx and his doctrines. Chapter VI concentrates on his early philosophical writings, where Marx struggles to find what poets today call his "voice," expressive both of his innermost yearnings and philosophical aspirations. In Chapter VII, I explore the way the young Marx moved to his materialist interpretation of history, his major contribution, transforming the way we look at any society. *Capital* is alleged to be Marx's most scientific statement, and in Chapter VIII I examine it carefully.

The penultimate chapter, IX, raises the question, If, as a social scientist, his theories are presumed to stand on their own, independent of their etiology, what difference does it make who Karl Marx actually was? In my answer, I find it necessary to touch on the related question of what is involved in the effort to construct a social science (a question I hope to make central in some future book). In seeking to understand Marx's contribution to the social sciences, surely it is essential to reflect on their nature and meaning. Thus, I attempt in this chapter to make a general statement, with implications both for Marx and beyond him. (I might add that my attention to Marx's individuality is not in terms of a psychohistorical study. Such a study, unlike this one, aims at a systematic application of specific psychological concepts and theories to its subject. I must also add that I cannot imagine any historical treatment, mine included, that is not informed by a particular sort of psychological understanding.)

The conclusion, Chapter X, seeks to sum up the book and to assess the major thrusts of Marx's life and work. In a short Epilogue, I strike a more personal note, and ponder the relevance of Marxism, as well as capitalism, to the condition of the world today.

Such are the goals of this book. The reader now has the signposts in front of him or her as to how I shall try to reach these goals.

I wish also to make more explicit than in the outline given above four leading theses, which emerge from what I have to say about Marx.

The first is that Marx must be viewed steadily in the context of his time, the early industrial revolution. Theological Marxists debate endlessly about the fine points of Marxist thought, as a closed system, never looking beyond the master to the reality which he purports to describe and analyze. I believe that such an attitude is not only inappropriate in itself but violates Marx's own injunction to think critically. I have tried, therefore, to bear steadily in mind the 19th-century industrial context and not just the Hegelian philosophical milieu, as I worried over Marx's meaning.

My second thesis is that Marx was very much a religious thinker, even though his thought takes the form of a secular religion, and, even more to the point, that it was his Christian upbringing that supplied him with his world view (in the form, or transformation, subsequently, of the Hegelian critique of religion), rather than his Jewish background. The Jewish heritage was important; but more for psychological than for intellectual reasons.

My third thesis is a corollary to the second: Marx did try, as well, to be scientific, i.e., to be a social scientist, but his effort was twisted by his millennial leanings. Paradoxically, the latter preserved him from being a simple positivist, and thus allowed him to envision a social science in which "what should be" mixed with "what is", i.e., where *praxis* is intentionally related to theory. Though in the end Marx betrayed his own insight, his effort stands as a potent inspiration for all of us today.

My last thesis does involve me, overtly, in one of those controversies to which I adverted earlier. As between those who see a unity holding together what has come to be called the young and the old Marx and those who see a break, I stand with the former. Where I differ from them, however, is in my evaluation of this unity. The "unity" scholars frequently view the young, humanist Marx as having been betrayed by followers, such as Lenin and Stalin, who stress the later, scientific Marx. The arid totalitarian outcomes of Marxism in our time, according to many neo-Marxists, can be redeemed or avoided by a return to the humanist Marx. I, alas, cannot share this view. As I read Marx, the unity of his thought insures that the same problems adhere in the humanist Marx as in the scientific Marx; it is only the language that he uses that is different (a position I spell out in this book). The way must be forward, past Marx, not backwards, to a pure Marx.

I do not present these theses particularly as arguments in my text. Rather, I hope that they emerge from my detailed effort to puzzle out the meaning of Marx's life and work. In the process, I trust that I do not obscure the fact that Marx was a lusty individual, compelling our admiration for his struggle with the important human issues of his time, and ours, whether we agree with his particular results or not. There is a drama to the life, aside from the doctrines themselves. That, surely, is also one of the meanings of Karl Marx, joining with the others I have sought to focus on in this book.

I

Why Marx?

Karl Marx's influence has been prodigious. Those who call themselves or are labeled Marxists number almost half the planetary inhabitants. The Chinese alone account for one billion, though the 260–80 million Russians claim to be the leading apostles. All in all, between 1.5 and 2 billion people are being led by dedicated Marxists, are being educated in Marxist thought, and thus can be classified as Marxists of one sort or another.

Marx's so-called "followers" outnumber those of the largest existing religious bodies: Christianity, Buddhism, and Islam.[1] Their numbers are great—but not as great as the Marxists. Marxism, the "secular religion" of the modern era, extends its sway over a population enormously swollen by the "Demographic Revolution" of the 18th to 20th century. Even allowing for this fact, however, Marxism has come to hold sway over more hearts and minds, or at least to dominate the ideologies of those in power in proportionately more parts of the world than any one of the major historical religions.*

* How, the reader might well ask, can I call Marxism a "religion," even a "secular" one?. Religion, especially in its Judeo-Christian form, embodies a belief in God and the supernatural, an afterlife, and so forth. Naturally, so defined, Marxism cannot be considered a religion. If, however, one looks at the *functions* of religion, especially its psychological functions, its offer of a total explanation of history, its messianic sense of time, its escha-

The great world religions all formed around some founding figure: a mythical Buddha, a vague Jesus, or a Muhammad just barely emerging from the shadows into the light of empirical detail. In contrast, Marx's life and work was to a large extent available to his contemporaries in an era—the 19th century—when historical science was blooming. Today the details of his existence and thoughts have become increasingly available to scholars and observers. A real Karl Marx, not a mythical figure, is available to us if we go in search of him.

Hegel, Marx's mentor, spoke of "spiritual revolutions" that silently occurred in the "spirit of the age," before bursting, like a bud, into actuality. In his so-called anti-theological writings, Hegel cites Abraham and Jesus, along with Alexander the Great and Caesar, as world-historical heroes, progenitors of revolutions. Marx was more like a Jesus than a Caesar, conquering with scriptures rather than swords. His role was one of prophecy rather than armed conquest. Yet the end result of his prophecy was a chain of explosive revolutions in Russia, China, Eastern Europe, Latin America, and elsewhere—of a magnitude unheard of in earlier times.

II

The German philosopher, Karl Jaspers, has spoken of the periods when the great world religions arose as "axial periods".[3] At such times, there is a "revolution" in the conditions of human existence and society turns on its axis. A new society emerges, whose legitimacy is validated in a new religion, which brings order out of social chaos and gives meaning to the flux of events.

The Industrial Revolution has been such a time. It is, I suggest, the most recent "axial period." And Marxism is its major new "religion,"

tological vision of a conflict between the forces of good and evil, and its hope for a complete regeneration of man, then Marxism can indeed qualify as a religion; it is in this sense that I call it a "secular religion," a sense that will be made clearer and, I hope, more convincing in the rest of this book.[2]

I am also aware that many of the 1.5 to 2 billion or so "followers" may be unwilling ones. Many Poles, Hungarians, etc., and even Russians, detest the Communist system. Nevertheless, their children are brought up in the new "faith," the public ceremonies are Marxist, etc. In the early years, not all those brought under the Christian or Islamic religions were willing converts, either. Yet, they have been considered as "adherents" of these faiths by historians.

emerging as a sect of capitalism. We are so close to the Industrial Revolution that we do not, perhaps, perceive its true dimensions. Between, say, 1760 and 1850 or 1860, a major transformation in human social evolution took place, equivalent to the Agricultural Revolution of ten thousand years ago. In increasing numbers in England, for example, men and women lived in towns and cities; as the 1851 census showed, a majority of the population no longer lived in rural areas. Increasingly also they worked in factories. Although factory workers were at no time numerically dominant—for example, they were outnumbered by agricultural laborers, domestic servants, artisans, etc.—they were, symbolically, the leading edge of the labor force. Machines became ubiquitous and were frequently thought to be omnipotent. A crucial breakthrough in standard of living occurred, first in England, and then later in the other industrialized countries, and economic expansion took on a self-sustaining and continuous quality. Man now became "industrial man" and, society, "industrial society."

This transformation, which we call "industrialization," or "modernization" (or sometimes "Westernization") and which can occur in any society, first took place in a specific historical form, in a particular place, and at a certain point in time: Great Britain in the mid-18th to 19th centuries and, to a lesser degree and a few decades later, France, America, Belgium, and elsewhere in the West.[4] It occurred, therefore, in a particular culture and society, which, in turn, indelibly colored the initial and most important responses to the great transformation. Once these responses were in place, they helped shape all other responses, in different countries and different times.

It is of great significance that the political context of the Industrial Revolution was the French Revolution, which "accidentally" occurred at roughly the same time. The phrase "Industrial Revolution" was first used by various French writers, especially Jérôme-Adolphe Blanqui in the late 1830s. It was coined in analogy to the local, Western phenomenon of the French Revolution, which, by different means—the political—was also perceived as creating a new society. "Industrialism" and "industrial society" were neologisms, fresh minted by Thomas Carlyle in *Sartor Resartus* (1833).

The initial period of the "Industrial Revolution" and the initial conditions of the first "industrialized society"—early 19th-century England—were desperate and difficult ones, especially at certain points on the newly emerging business cycle. Waves of unemployment, of want, and of misery struck at the new class, the proletariat, in the burgeoning new factory towns, such as Manchester, with their hideous slums, their lack of sanitation, and their overcrowding. The "condition of England," in its industrial rags, shocked observers ranging from Charles Dickens to Frederick Engels (whose *Condition of the Working-Class in England* [1845] was a graphic portrait of the dismal conditions). The "Hungry Forties" especially impressed itself on men's perceptions of the new industrial society, even though, as it happens, it was the watershed before conditions for an increasing proportion of the population began intermittently to improve.

In this "axial period" of great stress and change, with connections to the past being snapped and strained, the way was opened to new "religions." Not unexpectedly, with old values afloat, men grasped for new supports. Such religions frequently took the form of secular ideologies, though often efforts at reform and renewal of old religions were initial responses to the vicissitudes of industrialization. Thus, for example, Methodism can be seen as a renewed effort of Christianity to afford solace and psychological means of coping with the unprecedented conditions of industrial society. Even the supposedly secular ideologies, however, viewed more closely, carried powerful religious elements within them.[5]

In fact, much of the thought of the period can also be seen as the secularization of religious impulses: Providence is replaced by Adam Smith's Invisible Hand, operating in the market; God by Hegel's Reason, making itself manifest in history; and so forth.** Directly, or indirectly, in the name of religion or opposed to it, often in the form of science, the ideologies and social sciences of industrial society themselves verged on being eschatologies, millennial visions of man's emergence from the dislocations of this new, axial period.

Almost all observers were agreed on the fact that great and rapid change was taking place, but they disagreed in their evaluations of the results, and, if these were seen as degrading, what form amelioration should take. I have already referred to the Methodist reaction: it was along the lines of "if you can't beat them [the capitalists], join them," i.e., embrace the hard-working, frugal ethos of the Protestant Ethic. It was in the form of

---

** Although there are overlaps, secularization of religious impulses is not necessarily—and generally will not be—the same as a secular religion. The latter offers a total system, demanding total belief in the whole, whereas the former need only metamorphose particular elements from the religious past into a new secular form.

Methodism that this ethos was adopted by lower-middle class people. Another interesting religious response can be seen in Elizabeth Gaskell's *Mary Barton*. Its preachment was that even if the evils of the Industrial Revolution could not be prevented, their results could be softened and made bearable by Christian love of one another. It was published in 1848, the same year as *The Communist Manifesto*. Subtitled "A Tale of Manchester Life," it was written by the wife of a Unitarian minister, who lived in the pulsing factory city and had first-hand and prolonged experience of its horrors. Its hero, if one there is besides Mary, is John Barton, her father, a weaver out of work who "became a Chartist, a Communist, all that is commonly called wild and visionary." Although Gaskell is opposed to the class conflict preached by "Communists" (Gaskell does not mean Marxists, of which she knew almost nothing), she applauds their motives: "Ay! but being visionary is something. It shows a soul, a being not altogether sensual; a creature who looks forward for others, if not for himself." The proletariat, she realizes, is like a Frankenstein creation: "Why have we made them what they are; a powerful monster, yet without the inner means for peace and happiness?"

In terms that sound like those of Marx, Gaskell focuses on "the most deplorable and enduring evil that arose out of the period of commercial depression to which I refer . . . this feeling of alienation between the different classes of society." It is her solution, however, that exposes the gulf between the two observers: it would be best for all classes "that the truth might be recognized that the interests of one were the interests of all; and as such, required the consideration and deliberation of all; that hence it was most desirable to have educated workers, capable of judging, not mere machines of ignorant men; and to have them bound to their employers by the ties of respect and affection, not by mere money bargains alone; in short, to acknowledge the Spirit of Christ as the regulating law between both parties." Not the encouragement of class conflict, but its healing by a religion of love is Elizabeth Gaskell's response to the travail of industrialization.

Religion in its traditional, Christian dress, however, was itself under attack. In fact, it was one of the old values crumbling under the impact of the new forces. Intellectually, the so-called higher criticism, calling into account the revelatory features of the Old and New Testaments, was undermining belief in the old system of thought. Hegelianism was the most extreme development of this current, washing away in its left-wing form for many what was left of the bastions of religion.

Another response to industrial society is illustrated in the case of Thomas Carlyle, who so powerfully influenced Marx and every other critic of the new conditions. Unable to retain his faith in his natal Calvinism (as Gaskell did in Unitarianism), Carlyle agonized his way to a vague and shadowy substitute. He sought to transform religion, as society had been transformed, and to criticize the excesses of the Industrial Revolution from a secular perspective; but the traditional religious imagery remains. Unlike Marx, he did not adopt science as the new form of religion. Thus, in his essay "Characteristics" (1831), Carlyle declared, "The beginning of Inquiry is Disease: All Science . . . is and continues to be but Division, Dismemberment, and partial healing of the wrong. Thus, as was of old written, the Tree of Knowledge springs from a root of evil, and bears fruits of good and evil. Had Adam remained in paradise, there had been no Anatomy and no Metaphysics . . . The memory of that first state of Freedom and paradisaic Unconsciousness has faded away into an ideal poetic dream."

By the time of *Past and Present* (1843), Carlyle was hammering away at the theme of alienation and the need for the reintegration of industrial society. This theme had already been announced by the early Scottish Enlightenment thinkers, such as Adam Smith and Adam Ferguson. As early as 1767, the latter had warned that in a "commercial state . . . man is sometimes found a detached and a solitary being" who deals with his fellow men "for the sake of the profits they bring." Smith and Ferguson called attention to alienation as a blemish in the industrial and laissez-faire economy, while approving of the economy's main features. Carlyle, ambivalent about the new industrial powers loosed on the world, blasted its evil results. He attacked the turn to "Egoism," which he saw as the cause of division and isolation, and thundered in pulpit-like tones against "our present system of Mammonism, and Government by laissez-faire." In words that would be echoed by Marx, Carlyle condemned a society in which "cash payment is . . . the sole nexus of man with man," maintaining that "love of men cannot be bought by cash-payment; and without love men cannot endure to be together."

Carlyle appears to be halfway between Elizabeth Gaskell and the socialist critics (who were generally also anti-religious) of the alienating industrial society. A whole host of sectarian socialists emerged in the early 19th century—there is a good but one-sided account of them in *The Communist Manifesto*—and ranged themselves under the banners of Robert Owen, Charles Fourier, the Saint-Simonians, and innumerable others. Some accepted industrialism and the factory system, others opposed it; some were scientific in tone, others anti-scientific, if not religious; some sought a solution in rule by the managers, others by the masses; some were communitarian, or small-scale in their ideal society, others centralized. It would take another book to recount their schemes.

Marx was only one among these "Essenes" of early socialism. Each of his doctrines can be found, individually, in a rival sectarian. Some, in combination, can occasionally be found in one or more of his rivals. Obviously, the unique synthesis, the original version of Marxism, is his alone. Why did Marxism and not one of the other variants of socialism eventually become the ideology—the secular religion—which, in a kind of delayed reaction, for Marxism did not really spread until the last quarter of the 19th century, gripped the hearts and minds of multitudes of people experiencing the trauma of the axial period we know as the Industrial Revolution? Why, indeed, are we all Marxists, even those who are violently anti-Marxist, in the sense that Karl Marx has largely defined the terms in which we discuss and analyze the experience that members of the human species first underwent in England during the years 1760 to 1850?

III

It is generally said—Engels is probably the first to put it in this light—that Marx's appeal rested on his explosive fusion of Hegelian dialectics, English classical political economy, and French revolutionary socialism. To this mix, one should add Scottish sociology and Continental Romanticism. It is, indeed, a powerful brew. We need, however, to look more closely at some of the ingredients.

It was not just that Marx drew on classical economic theory. More to the point is that, unlike many of his competitors in revolution, Marx fully accepted the developing economic world around him, the work of the bourgeoisie, as the foundation of his future society. He did not reject the Industrial Revolution, as did a Charles Fourier, a Pierre-Joseph Proudhon, a Jean-Jacques Rousseau, or a Henry David Thoreau, but posited its powerful productive forces, resulting in increased wealth, as the foundation of communism. Thus, he aligned himself with the economic reality, the forces of the future, which he criticized using classical economic theory. Seen in this fashion, Marx can be viewed as the last of the great classical economists (he accepts Smith's labor theory of value, Ricardo's putative iron law of wages, etc.), who then becomes the leading heretic in preaching a "reformation."

The Saint-Simonians, too, accepted the Industrial Revolution. But, like their fellow Comteans, they placed their emphasis on the power of ideas, of conversion (both Saint-Simon, and his erstwhile disciple, Comte, ended up advocating a "religion of humanity"), rather than of economic forces to bring about change. Marx, with his theory of the economic determinism of history, could claim a different engine puffing toward change in society, one which could be analyzed as operating in accord with scientific laws. The laws of thermodynamics would have their counterpart in the world of men as well as of molecules. Thus, Marx embraced not only the Industrial Revolution itself, but also the scientific spirit in back of it; or so he claimed.

Again, where the Saint-Simonians looked to an elite of bankers, industrialists and scientists to guide the new society, Marx, in the democratic spirit of the French Revolution, turned to the masses. He did not see them, as most of the French revolutionary socialists did, as "the people," or the sans-culottes, but as the "proletariat," as much a "product" of industrialism as its textiles and railroads.

Blanquists, for example, set themselves up as the heirs to the Jacobin tradition of the French Revolution. That meant that they wished to return to a pre-industrial world of artisans and shopkeepers, imbued with republicanism and infused with a new kind of nationalism. It meant that their gaze was, fundamentally, fixed on the past, even if a recent one.

Marx's ideal, and his ideas, were of the future. He made the new factory workers his hero. Instead of republicanism, a bourgeois ideal, Marx projected communism; instead of nationalism, he held aloft the banner of internationalism (which had the advantage of being in tune with the emerging world market, i.e., the true forces of economic growth, though Marx may have badly judged the actual political stituation of his own time); where the Blanquists thought in terms of riots and revolution in the streets, Marx (though attracted from time to time by such a form of action) recognized his epoch as one marked by the beginning of mass parties, and placed his bets on the proletariat.

Again, unlike some of the unrevolutionary socialists, such as Robert Owen or Charles Fourier, who preached "harmony," Marx exhorted the masses in the name of "conflict." He appealed directly to the anger and aggression of the workers, justifying their struggle, whether they used violent or parliamentary means. What is more, Marx took a direct role in the actual revolutionary movement, seeking to impose the stamp of both his ideas and his personality on, for example, the uprisings of 1848 (Marx was unsuccessful in this attempt) and the International Working Men's Association of 1864.

When we speak of English classical political economy as being one of the elements in Marx's protean synthesis, then we must conceive of it in the broadest terms, such as outlined above. It is not only the theory, but the action, or *praxis*, of economics, shaping and interpreting the emerging world of industrialism, that Marx had in mind as he went about his task of forecasting and constructing his future communist society.

IV

Marx could lay claim to being a social scientist as well as a socialist. After all, economics, increasingly his favorite study, puts itself forward as the most scientific of the social sciences; and, as Marx interpreted the Hegelian dialectic, it, too, when made materialistic (idealism stood on its head), was "scientific," i.e., provided one with the "laws" of history. We shall see later in this book, in detail, how Marx used Hegelian critique to develop his positive science. However, if we continue to focus here on Marx's life and work as a response to the axial transformation of the Industrial Revolution, we suddenly realize that he is responding to it, not only "scientifically" (a response to be looked at more closely), but apocalyptically, i.e., in religious terms.

The particular form of Marx's religious millennialism is Romantic. As M. H. Abrams points out, we have generally been unaware "of the full extent to which characteristic concepts and patterns of Romantic philosophy and literature are a displaced and reconstituted theology, or else a secularized form of devotional experience. . . ."[6] Marx, whose early writings were highly Romantic, and who devoted so much of his youthful powers to a critique of religion, was certainly unconscious of his heritage in this regard. Pierre-Joseph Proudhon, one of his rival socialist sectarians, himself an advocate of "Humanitarian Atheism," was more aware how steeped in religious imagery, language, views, and inspirations he was and acknowledged: "[I am] forced to proceed as a materialist, that is to say, by observation and experience, and to conclude in the language of a believer, because there exists no other; not knowing whether my formulas, theological despite myself, ought to be taken as literal or as figurative . . . We are full of the Divinity, *Jovis omnia plena*; our monuments, our traditions, our laws, our ideas, our languages, and our sciences—all are infected with this indelible superstition, outside of which we are not able either to speak or act, and without which we simply do not think."

Abrams labels what was going on in the early 19th century "Natural Supernaturalism" (Carlyle's phrase in *Sartor Resartus*), where the tendency was "to naturalize the supernatural and to humanize the divine." Faced with the breakdown of values, epitomized in the constant lament over the lack of "connection," the Romantic enterprise was to rescue the cultural tradition of the past by reconstituting it in terms of the new. In executing this task, the Romantics also resurrected the doctrine of a fall from grace, followed by absolute revolution, and the creation of a new man in a new Heaven (only in this case, earth).

In his more than 500 pages of closely woven text, Abrams sustains his general argument to this effect. He summarizes the features of Romantic millennial belief, which modeled itself on Christian example, as follows (and I quote in full, though it is a long list):

> The doctrine and trial of a total revolution, which is conceived to possess many, or all, of these attributes: (1) the revolution will, by an inescapable and cleansing explosion of violence and destruction, reconstitute the existing political, social, and moral order absolutely, from its very foundations, and so (2) bring about abruptly, or in a remarkably short time, the shift from the present era of profound evil, suffering, and disorder to an era of peace, justice, and optimal conditions for general happiness; (3) it will be led by a militant elite, who will find ranged against them the forces dedicated to preserving the present evils, consolidated in a specific institution or class or race; (4) though it will originate in a particular and critical time and place, it will by irresistible contagions spread every where, to include all mankind; (5) its benefits will endure for a very long time, perhaps forever, because the transformation of the institutional circumstances and cultural ambience of man will help the intellectual and spiritual malaise which has brought him to his present plight; and (6) it is inevitable, because it is guaranteed either by a transcendent or by an immanent something, not ourselves, which makes for the ineluctable triumph of total justice, community, and happiness on earth.

We quickly recognize many of these attributes in the Marxist revolution (indeed, Abrams, though devoting most of his book to Wordsworth, has a few pages specifically devoted to showing Marx's role in the development of "Natural Supernaturalism"). What Marx did was to fuse Romantic apocalyptic thinking with classical economic thought, adding Hegelian elements as well. He then presented his millennial "religious" thought in "scientific" guise. His "science," it turns out, is, actually, a secularization of a number of Judeo-Christian notions. Like another Jew before him, who converted to a faith of his own making, Marx became the founder of a new, world-wide religion, which is named after him: in this case, Marxism, instead of Christianity (Jesus' name becoming Jesus Christ). (The fact that both religions, though founded by Jews, have lent themselves on occasion to antisemitic purposes is one of the ironies of history.)

As is well known, Marx appealed not only to economic science, but invoked the name of Darwin as an analogy to his own role in discovering the laws, not of "natural technology," but of "human technology." As Marx saw it, both men were scientists, studying the animal man. In Marx's confident words: "Would not the history of human technology be easier to write than the history of natural technology?"[7] On the contrary, I am asserting that Marx's "science" is a modern, secular form of religious apocalyptic thinking—"natural supernaturalism"—and is as close, in a way, to Christian Science, as it is to Darwin's science.

Darwin, with his theory of evolution by natural selection, marked a sharp discontinuity, even though here and there religious remnants hung on, with the modes and categories of theological thinking. If Darwin was the break with the 19th century's secularization of religion, Marx was its culmination. His secular "theology", the endless arguments over fine points of Marxist dogma, so dear to Marxist exegetes, made and make him appealing to intellectuals (it is an appeal similar to that of James Joyce for other scholars). Best of all, devoted Marxists can have their religion and pretend it is science. As for the masses, less concerned with any serious pretense to science, though reassured that Marxism is "scientific," they can embrace a "religion" of atheism, with all the rituals, ceremonies, symbolic representations, and mythic claims immanent in traditional religion. Such connection to the old, in the name of the new, is a prime reason for Marxism's appeal that is not to be scoffed at.

With Marxism, moreover, the Christian torments of the soul over its salvation are superseded by a concern for living in accord with Marxist

orthodoxy. Damnation takes place on this earth, where one is cast out
of the Party on being found guilty of having overstepped the Party line,
since there is no longer a Heaven in which the drama of division between God's and Satan's souls can take place (this party line development is not in Marx's own writings, but in Marxism as it developed as
a theology).

In seeking to account for why Marx and not some other socialist became the major founder of an ideology emerging from the industrial
transformation of the early 19th century, we must place his "scientific
religious" appeal very high. It was deeply rooted in his own personal
development, as I shall try to show. It was in accord with the climate
of opinion established by Auguste Comte and his Positivism (character-
istically, Marx rejected Comte while using some of the same ideas). It
combined with Marx's Romantic inspiration, expressed in his powerful
and moving prose, which was itself a form of poetry. His words and lines
hum in our ears as much as do those of Wordsworth or Byron. Marx
saw history as a form of drama, and he encapsulated his vision in dramatic terms. Both the religious and the sheer imaginative appeal are
missed by the Marxist exegetes in their theological disquisitions.

When we add to these facets of his appeal the fact that he accepted
"positively" the new economic forces gathering around him, that he
synthesized the leading intellectual filaments of his epoch and applied
them to the emerging industrial world, and that one result was, in fact,
lasting contributions, once shorn of their holistic setting, to social science, i.e., to the way we look at and try to analyze the structure and
dynamics of society, then we can readily see some of the reasons why
Marxism ultimately became the response of choice for so many. At the
time, one could not have predicted that it would win out so triumphantly. After the event, we can see the reasons why.

In emphasizing Marx's religious appeal, I do not mean to underestimate the cognitive attraction of his work. He did address real social
problems—the dislocations of the Industrial Revolution as well as what
he saw as the innate flaws of capitalism. He also sought to understand
the flux of historical events by designing a social analysis that would lend
itself to objective discourse. Thus, his appeal was, and is, cognitive as
well as religious, intellectual as well as emotional, and on the terrain of
"what is" as well as "what should be." It is a universal appeal exactly
because of its protean aspects. And because there are so many motives
for being a Marxist, the question of which one achieves primacy in any

given instance becomes an empirical—I would say historical—problem; with the result being that Marxist revolutions are of very different types and outcomes, for reasons of motive as well as circumstance.[8]

I am also arguing that in Marx himself the cognitive and emotional were fused, and are only artificially separable, and that this is a necessary condition of creative work in social science (see further Chapter IX). Our personal response to Marx tends to be in the same terms: while parts of Marx's analysis are, in principle, either conflict-free psychologically, or detachable from Marxism philosophically, like stones taken out of water, they lose much of their luster for us when removed from his total system. The spread of Marxism, as a movement, as distinct from particular ideas of Marx about social analysis, cannot be attributed to its cognitive as detached from what I am calling its religious appeal, even when Marxists declare otherwise and call themselves atheists. I hope to make clear in the chapters that follow why this is so, while giving full weight to the cognitive appeal and value of Marx's work.

V

All the great monotheistic religions were largely rural in their origin and basic appeal (although in the end representing the victory of the city and a centralized ruler). Their paradises were a return to a garden of Eden or a Bedouin delight. Marx's "religion" was from the beginning, as befits a creative response to the Industrial Revolution, an urban phenomenon. Its chosen people were the factory workers of the new towns— Marx scorned the peasants as backward and uncouth—and its apostles in the late 19th–early 20th centuries were the students and scholars of the universities, whose outlook, even if not their origin, was citified. Paradoxically, the paradise was a return to the garden of Eden, though the purgatory to be passed through was industrialization.

We have already noted the reasons for Marxism's appeal in the West. Yet, as we know, it did not really triumph there. While Marxist parties arose, and occasionally, in the form of social democrats, came to power, they did not bring about a successful communist revolution in Western Europe (or America). Capitalist reform, not communist revolution, has prevailed up until now. The capitalist structure and values that had made possible the Industrial Revolution in the West have held firm there, paradoxically, aided by the push to reform from working class and socialist forces, and have allowed the existing societies to cope.

The varied fortunes of Marxism in the West depended upon the accidents of organization, wars, depressions, internal politics, chance leaders, and other such features of any movement. Because, in an historical sense, the Marxist "religion" has been oriented to the future and has sought to grapple with the actual reality of emerging industrialism in different countries, its characteristic mode of adaptation has been revisionism. In Western Europe, reformism or revisionism, not revolution, was the alternative to capitalism (which we must also view as having an ideology, i.e., being a secularized religion, though with nothing like the apocalyptic features of Marxism: the idea of progress is the closest approximation).

Marx's fate, in fact, was to be a prophet outside his own land, in the sense that only in non-Western parts of the world did Marxist regimes come to power, converting millions of people to the new orthodoxy. The spread of Marxism is analogous to the expansion of Christianity and Islamism. While major differences exist, what is spectacularly evident is that Marxism spread in the period from 1917 to 1949 over vast areas of the earth and over huge numbers of people in a manner reminiscent of the crusading religions. The comparable expansion is that of the Muslim faith, which after its foundation in Muhammad's visions around 610 took on conversional and organizational form at Mecca about fifteen years later and then raced through Syria, Mesopotamia, Palestine and Egypt by 642 and then, as Islam, went on to the conquest of Northern Africa and Spain. By the 8th century, Islamism reigned as a dominant religion from the Atlantic Ocean to the Himalayas.

The beginning of the real spread of the Marxist "religion" dates from the Revolution of 1917 in Russia. It is odd that Marx, the founder of what we can now view as a great secular "religion," was so convinced that economics was the only real determinant of history. He appears to have been totally unconscious of the religious appeal of his own Marxism. Yet Marxism first succeeded in religious-believing Russia, a backward country where the capitalist industrialization required by Marx's "scientific socialism" had not yet developed. Lenin was the charismatic leader, gifted with extraordinary organizational abilities, who played the St. Paul, as well as the St. Peter, to Marx, and, adjusting Marxism to existing conditions, made a successful revolution in its name. Moscow then became the Mecca from which Marxism, in its new version, radiated outwards.

The story of Marxism's spread is a major part of modern history. Its more successful expansion in the non-Western parts of the world—*in partibus infidelibus*—depended initially on the same factors I enumerated in discussing its less successful manifestations in the West. Whole libraries have been devoted to its rise to power in Russia, China, and elsewhere. I have no intention of recapitulating any of this work. Nor, here, do I want to deal with the question of how true to Marx's own views a particular Marxist party may be; as Marx himself remarked, aghast at what some of his followers were making of him, "Je ne suis pas marxist". Suffice it to say, as with any religious or ideological movement, different times and different places can make for strange twists in the basic fabric of belief.

I do wish to hint, however, at the kind of reasons one might adduce for why Marx, and not another prophet, was chosen by a people or its leaders. In all cases, the answer must be looked for in a combination of the general appeal of Marxism, as I have sketched it, and its fit and adaptation to local conditions. For example, in Russia, authoritarian orthodoxy (the Czar and the Russian Orthodox Church) could find its continuation in a new and updated form: a version of Marxism which emphasized the authoritarian, apocalyptic strands in Marx. Lenin was the genius who realized that the small, secret band of Bolsheviks could rule in the name of the proletariat—"The dictatorship of the proletariat"—as they sought to guide the Soviet Union through the stages of industrialization—"Soviets plus electrification" is how Lenin defined communism. For him and his successors, such as Stalin, science, i.e., "scientific socialism," could replace the religion of an Alexander III as the legitimizing agent for their exercise of power. Marxist-Leninism became the way of coping in Russia with the axial transformation of industrial revolution.

In even less well-developed countries exposed to Western imperialism, one might have expected Marxism to be rejected as a Western import. China is a good example of why this did not happen. The Celestial Kingdom was itself not religious: Confucianism was primarily a moral and political system. In orthodox Russia, the apocalyptic orthodoxy of Marxism—in the name of atheism—allowed for a connection of tradition with the new modes of industrializing society. In China, Marxist atheism, unlike Christianity, did not appear to impose an unwanted Western religious orthodoxy on the proud central kingdom, thereby forcing it to break with its non-religious tradition. Thus, Marxism could have it both ways. Moreover, Marxism as an acceptable "ideology" permitted China to appropriate the Industrial Revolution, and thus a kind of "Westernization" that, itself a product of capitalism, criticized and attacked Western capitalism and its imperialism.

Marxism's protean nature thus allowed it to appeal to two widely disparate countries and cultures, Russia and China. Mao Zedong, of course, was the Lenin of China, adapting Marx to his own country. If Lenin adapted the founder's ideas to a society where the bourgeoisie had not yet accomplished its assigned task, Mao went further and adapted them to a country without a significant proletariat. In fact, he glorified the peasants so scorned by Marx. Why, then, did Mao bother with Marx at all? The problem was how to modernize and industrialize China, while rejecting a capitalist ideology. China had no tradition of democracy; though Mao flirted for a short period of time with Western liberal ideas, he quickly abandoned them. Marxist-Leninism, with its justification of elite party rule in the drive to industrialization, justified the new mandarins of China. The very success of the Russian Revolution held out hope for a similar outcome in China.[9]

Within the Marxist ideology, Mao found the crucial ingredient of aggression needed to release the anger of the peasants against their overlords (and against Japan, for Mao fused communism with nationalism). Confucianism was passive and filial; Marxism was active and parricidal, justifying the rebellion against the established imperial, and subsequently republican, authority. So, too, an ideology of internationalism could be metamorphosed into a vehicle for national assertion by a great people who in earlier days had identified themselves with the center of the universe.

On the face of it, Marxism should not have appealed to China or fitted in with its needs. Marxism, although with some ambiguity on the matter, postulated a deterministic historical development, almost none of which had occurred in China. It originated in Western conditions of industrialization, praised the city against the countryside, talked of proletarians, while disparaging peasants, came on the shoulders of Western imperialism and internationalism, and spoke in an apocalyptic tradition foreign to China. Yet, as we know, it has become the official "religion," bracing and guiding China as it transforms itself from an agrarian to an industrialized society.

History is full of ironies. Ironies, however, looked at more closely, turn out to have a logic, though it is a logic of their own. We could, of course, dismiss the spread of Marxism as an accident. If so, it is a massive recurrent accident. It makes more sense, therefore, to view the rise and expansion of Marxism as a basically religious response—in modern terms, an ideology—to the experience of industrialization, taking varied and often very different shapes in different parts of the world. Detailed examination will reveal in each case why it is Marxism, and not some other world view and value-system, that appealed. In back of each such explanation, however, lies the original formulation of Marxism in all its protean aspects, and in back of the formulation lies the founder, Marx himself.

VI

In the beginning, communism was what ever Marx said it was. His depiction of its inevitable coming, and its idyllic nature once arrived, presumably defined its reality. Once a revolution in Marx's name occurred in Russia in 1917, and a communist society installed professing his ideas, another reality seemed to exist. Its apparent aberrations from his doctrines raised the question of what Marxist reality really is. A totalitarian and dogmatic Soviet Union could be dismissed as a false, or distorted, version of Marxism. When, however, other revolutionary Marxist movements rose to power around the world showing similar features, it became more difficult to reconcile the divergences between political reality and moral exhortation, between communism as it existed on some earth, and communism as it existed in Marx's eschatological vision.

It appears useful, then, to suggest a direction for a re-examination of Marx's vision, in order to see what connection there might really be between it and the communist societies actually generated in its name. Our task is not easy, for the connection between ideas and events is extremely difficult to discern. In the end, all we can probably speak of will be tendencies, whose final outcome must not be prejudged here.

In any discussion of future developments of Marxism, I think it helpful to remind ourselves of John Maynard Keynes's eloquent statement about the power of ideas: "The ideas of economists and political philosophers, both when they are right and when they are wrong, are more powerful than is commonly understood. Indeed the world is ruled by little else. Practical men, who believe themselves to be quite exempt from any intellectual influences, are usually the slaves of some defunct economist. Madmen in authority, who hear voices in the air, are distilling their frenzy from some academic scribbler of a few years back."[10] The fact is that, aside from his inconsequential attempts at revolutionary activity, Marx was an "academic scribbler." He needed the "Madmen in authority"—though I would amend this to "charismatic leaders"—to give force and material shape to his ideas. Without the Lenins and Maos of this world, where would Marxism be? It is they who, for all practical purposes, and for better or for worse, turn the output of Marx into Marxism as we know it, extrapolating, however, from Marx's own version.

Marx himself, in his better moments, pointed the way. He realized that new experience might and should modify his ideas. A science, though not a dogma, changes in the light of new evidence. Russian or Chinese communists might claim to be the "true Marxists," but, all communists, as I have shown, have in fact, had to move away from Marx. Mao Zedong, for example, recognized this fact boldly. In 1958, he openly discussed the "fear of Marx," arguing that one should go beyond Marx: "Do not be afraid, because Marx was also a human being, with two eyes, two hands, and one brain, not much different from us, except that he had a lot of Marxism in his mind." As Mao went on, new theories are required because "in our work of socialist construction, we are still to a large extent acting blindly. For us the socialist economy is still in many respects a realm of necessity not yet understood."[11] Even more dramatically, Mao proclaimed, "What we have done surpasses Marx. . . . Our practice surpasses Marx. Through practice, new principles are produced. Marx never succeeded in making revolution; we succeeded. The practice of this revolution, reflected in the form of consciousness, becomes theory."[12]

A further glance at that extraordinary figure, Mao Zedong, is in order here. He wrestled mightily, in theory and practice, with the contradictions in and between Marx and Chinese society. As a result, a Maoist embodiment of Marx took on a life of its own. As we also know, that Maoist legacy in China is itself being revised. Mao had tried, more than any other communist, to make real Marx's utopian aspirations. Now his successors are saying, "Let's be realistic", in a different sense, and are turning, *mirabile dictu*, to neo-classical economic formulations in a socialist, but not communist, framework.

Whatever the swings to and fro, past and to come, in Chinese Maoism-Marxism, it is clear that the utopian vision, if and when brought to earth, must always be adjusted to a particular society, a particular people, and a particular past.

What is more, it is less than a century since the first communist regime came to power. Marxism as the shaping ideology in a given society is a recent development. What sort of culture will it produce? For good or bad, communism is here to stay for the foreseeable future. (Like capitalism, the other ideology of the Industrial Revolution, it will someday pass from the stage of history, as feudalism did earlier.) Communism will take a different shape in Russia, China, Eastern Europe, Latin America, and elsewhere, depending on the local political atmosphere and the events of history. In each of these areas, it will mix with past traditions to produce a culture of its own. All of these cultures, however, whatever their differences, will be Marxist.

Christianity is ecumenical, although it varies enormously from Poland to Portugal, Lebanon to Brazil. The same can be said of Islamic countries. It took both of these world religions centuries until they worked out a recognizable Christian or Islamic culture. Chartres and the Alhambra, and the cultures that produced them, did not develop in a day. Who knows what forms of science and technology, customs and mores, communities and arts will be brought forth by Marxism? Historians are used to taking the long view, and the arid totalitarianism of contemporary communist countries may give way to a whole new form of human relatedness, consonant with the needs and aspirations of a society that has experienced the industrializing process. Or it may not. (Or, indeed, both communism and capitalism, and all the variants inbetween, may disappear in a nuclear cloud.)

All of this is the possible future. At the moment, we have only the actual present and the past. The past has shaped the present, and will shape the future. The past of Marxism starts with a man, Karl Marx. *** We know, and can know, a great deal about him. As I remarked at the beginning of this book, unlike other founders of great religions, Marx is not shrouded in the mists of time, but is a real, historical figure.

It is hard to remember that the father of scientific socialism was once a young boy and man. [14] All his pictures (with the exception of a sketch of him as a curly-haired, moustached university student) show him

*** [Frederick Engels, his life-long collaborator, accurately remarked, à propos of the *Communist Manifesto*, that the "basic thought belongs solely and exclusively to Marx"; the comment could serve more or less for the entire corpus of Marxism, which is why, without derogation to Engels, we can focus on the man who gave his name to their ideology. The role of Engels, however, as a financial and intellectual supporter of Marx— and, indeed, after his death, as a leading figure in the developing Marxist movement—is another matter. Independent of Marx, Engels deserves attention in his own right. [13]

bearded and old, or old before his time. He looks leonine—an old lion. But as his younger contemporary Wordsworth reminds us, "The child is father to the man." We cannot recover the child Marx—the historical materials are not available—but we can hope to see the "childish," or rather, "childlike" (in a positive sense) elements that persevere in him, and we can certainly recover the "young Marx."

In doing so, we need to bring a fresh eye to the task. Even so sage and knowledgeable a scholar as Isaiah Berlin misleads us when, aware though he is of the conflict between father and son manifested in the Marx correspondence, he concludes that "their relations continued to be warm, intimate and grave until the death of the older Marx in 1838."[15] I think a closer look will show that things are more complicated than that. It is also a "critical" eye, in the spirit of Marx's own use of critique, that we must bring to bear on the man and his work. For Marx *is* a man, we must remind ourselves. He is neither a demiurge, nor a devil, as some of his supporters or detractors would have us believe.

Among some Marxists (and especially in the East European communist states), a discussion has raged over what is called "Socialism with a Human Face." Its proponents argue that socialism in the Soviet Union and similar totalitarianisms is a distortion and a betrayal of Marxism. They go back to a "young Marx," the Marx of the early manuscripts, such as the recently published "Economic and Philosophic Manuscripts of 1844," and see a "humanist Marx" who would be shaken by the regimes now ruling in his name. The young, humanist Marx is opposed to an old, or mature, "scientific" (pseudo-scientific) Marx.[16] In the name of the earlier Marx they call for a "Reformation," to return communism to its pristine origin. The philosophical debate as to the nature of Marx and his work, consequently, has serious political implications.

I think it useful and enlightening to consider these matters under the title "Marx with a Human Face." In so doing, we can then subsume the arguments about a young and old, a humanist and a scientific Marx— "Socialism With a Human Face"—under this broader consideration. We need to concern ourselves with Marx the human, as well as with Marx the humanist. Before the latter comes the former. How else can we understand the real power and meaning of his work, humanist or scientific, except in the light of knowledge of the real, living human being, Karl Marx, as best we can know him historically? While Marxism the "religion" takes on a life—and thus a history—of its own, it all begins in the life of its originator. Marxism, I am arguing, is Marx writ large.

II

The Poetic Philosopher

The Philosopher-King was Plato's ideal; poets were to be banished from his realm. In political developments since his time, few if any philosopher-kings have ruled. Poets, however, even if ineffectually, have mixed with politics. One thinks of Byron in the Greek War of Independence or Alfred de Vigny celebrating the insurrection in Paris in July 1830. In general, however, poetry and politics are not seen as particularly compatible professions.

It may come as something of a surprise, therefore, to note that Marx was a poet before he became a philosopher and then a revolutionary. More to the point, to understand him in his latter roles, I claim that it is critical to look at him first in his poetic raiment.

The fact is that Marx's first published works were two poems in the Berlin *Athenaeum*, in 1841.[1] Written in 1837, they were included in a book of verse dedicated to his father. One, called "The Fiddler," speaks in Faust-like terms: "With Satan I have struck my deal./ He chalks the signs, beats time for me,/ I play the death march fast and free." The other, "Nocturnal Love," also sounds the death note: "You have drunk poison, Love./ With me you must away. The sky is dark above,/ No more I see the day."

The sentiments are typical of the romantic genre. Marx was about eighteen years old when he gave expression to them. He had already written "three volumes" of poems, which he had sent to his fiancée, Jenny, and which have not survived. We are more fortunate with another collection, which the author entitled *Book of Love*, followed by another, *Book of Songs*, which were dedicated to his beloved, Jenny, and later rededicated in part to his father as his father approached death. Some of the poems in this collection, while still typically romantic in their sentiments, strike a personal note as well, sounding themes that persist into later life and work. One particular poem, "Feelings", signals its personal importance and puts us directly in touch with the author's emotions by its title as well as its dedication to Jenny.

Let us reprint the major portion of this poem and read it together. It is not really a good poem, but its intensity of feeling works its effect on us:

> Never can I do in peace
> That with which my Soul's obsessed,
> Never take things at my ease;
> I must press on without rest.
>
> Others only know elation
> When things go their peaceful way,
> Free with self-congratulation,
> Giving thanks each time they pray.
>
> I am caught in endless strife,
> Endless ferment, endless dream;
> I cannot conform to Life,
> Will not travel with the stream.
>
> Heaven I would comprehend,
> I would draw the world to me;
> Loving, hating, I intend
> That my star shine brilliantly. . .
>
> . . . Worlds I would destroy for ever,
> Since I can create no world,
> Since my call they notice never,
> Coursing dumb in magic whirl.
>
> Therefore let us risk our all,
> Never resting, never tiring;
> Not in silence dismal, dull
> Without action or desiring;
>
> Not in brooding introspection
> Bowed beneath a yoke of pain,

> So that yearning, dream and action
> Unfulfilled to us remain.

The themes are clear; a new critic would turn aside, bored by their obviousness. The first note struck is that of "endless strife": the writer is in turmoil and pain. The next note informs us that the writer feels out of step, "alienated," we might say, from the world around him. He cannot conform; he wishes to be free to go his own way. Then comes the note of ambition: "I intend that my star shine brilliantly"—at whatever cost. And then the call to action: if the world will not notice him, i.e., respond to his ambition, then he will destroy it. The youthful poet's dreams will be fulfilled, but exactly with what content and how is left vague.

One feels a *Weltschmerz* in the author. The poem is filled with adolescent yearnings. With so many of his generation—the early 19th century—he is on the edge of "brooding introspection." The threat of depression hangs over the poem and its author. He turns, violently, to action to avoid his melancholy. Or at least he indicates that action is, or will be, his desired course.

What sort of action? He does not know as yet. Another of the poems, "To Jenny," gives us some hints. It is not the expected outpouring of love—that is contained in an accompanying poem, also entitled "To Jenny," which concludes, *"Love is Jenny, Jenny is Love's Name"*. The first "Jenny" poem is another matter. It is about words. It expresses the poet's frustration at having to pour his abounding spirits into dead words. Let us together read this poem, too:

> Words—lies, hollow shadows, nothing more,
>   Crowding Life from all sides round!
> In you, dead and tired, must I outpour
>   Spirits that in me abound?
> Yet Earth's envious Gods have scanned before
>   Human fire with gaze profound;
> And forever must the Earthling poor
>   Mate his bosom's glow with sound.
> For, if passion leaped up, vibrant, bold,
>   In the Soul's sweet radiance,
> Daringly it would your worlds enfold,
> Would dethrone you, would bring you down low,
>   Would oursoar the Zephyr-dance.
> Ripe a world above you then would grow.

The allusion to the "envious Gods" and "human fire" recalls to us the story of Prometheus, who defied the Gods and brought fire to mankind. The poet appears to be telling us that his words will be like fire and as a result will "dethrone" the Gods; and then create a world "above" them. Here we have the same theme of destroying the existing world, only now the means are indicated—words—and the action's result indicated—the creation of another world more to the poet's heart's desire (although what that may be is still not made clear).

The youthful poet struggles in another of his poems, "My World," to discern its lineaments. Even if he encompassed all the existing universe—"Drank I all the stars' bright radiance,/ All the light by suns o'erspilled," his pains would not be assuaged, and his dreams would remain unfulfilled. Above all existing worlds is "my own will," he declares. It drives him to "endless battle. . . . Demon-wise into the far mists driving/ Towards a goal I cannot near." Overcome by a feeling of hopelessness, he turns suddenly in the remainder of the poem to his Jenny and in her eyes finds an answer: she and the All are one.

It is not an answer that the rest of the collected poems makes convincing. Love, and Jenny, are the solid moorings for the author as he moves out into the confusing and disturbing world around him, but his will is clearly driving him forward, to both destruction and creation. Demon, or God, it is not clear on which side he is arraigning himself. The demons, of course, are also gods, as a mention of Satan reminds us. Will the poet be a Satan, a Prometheus in the Greek version, defying the gods? And what would this mean?

We have other fragmentary works from our aspiring author. At about the same time as his poems, he was also writing a play *Oulanem*, and a "humoristic," or satirical, novel, *Scorpion and Felix*.[2] As literary works, they are dreadful. Unlike the poems, they are obscure, crabbed, "clever," and utterly uninspired. They were wisely left unfinished, and unpublished (as, indeed, were the poems). And we would be equally wise to leave them uninterpreted, not bothering to seek a further understanding of our youthful poet in them.

II

Marx wrote his poetry in the late 1830s, at a time when the romantic inspiration ran high and the "Young Germans" were prominent. Three of them—Heinrich Heine, Ferdinand Freiligrath, and Georg Herwegh—became especially involved with the revolutionary turmoil of their time and with Marx. For example, Heine, inspired by Marx, wrote *Germany, A Winter's Tale* in 1844, which he described in a letter to Marx as "This radical, revolutionary . . . poem." The millennial note is sounded when Heine declaims:

> A new song, a better song,
> My friends, I will sing to you:
> We mean now, here on earth,
> To build the Kingdom of heaven.

Its revolutionary aspect is announced in the next stanza, as Heine continues to sing:

169	We mean to be happy on earth,
170	And to toil no longer.
171	The lazy bully shall not squander
-173	What industrious hands have wrought.[3]

Sympathetic to Marx, Heine cannot be said to have been a very knowledgeable student of Marxism; his sentiments are the conventional ones of his time.

Herwegh and Freiligrath, though more directly involved with Marx's revolutionary activities, in the end proved less docile pupils than Heine. Annoyed at their hesitation in accepting his direction, Marx subsequently broke with both of them. Freiligrath's protest at the time of the 1848 revolution in Germany to being yoked to Marx's political demands is worth quoting: "My nature, and that of any poet, needs freedom! Even the party is a kind of cage and one can sing better out of it than in, even when one is singing *for* the party . . . So I want to continue standing on my own feet, I want to belong only to myself and have sole responsibility for myself!"[4]

In fact, Freiligrath was voicing the central Romantic conviction of autonomy and spontaneous freedom, a version of which we have seen asserted in Marx's own early poems. We face a paradox. Marx's romantic and idealist inspirations come into conflict with his revolutionary aspirations. The humanist-scientific ambiguity of Marx's mind and soul is already implicit in any consideration of his relations to poetry, his own and others.

At the time he was writing his own poetry, Marx was not particularly concerned with the miserable lot of the workers but rather with the Romantic anguish over the growing quantification and objectification of life as a result of capitalism and science. Marx's sentiments, therefore, were initially pre-capitalist in their coloring, hardly differing in this regard from conservative critics. As Edmund Burke, an unlikely ally at first glance, had remarked, "The age . . . [was one of] sophisters, economists, and calculators."

Keats spoke of Newton "unweaving the rainbow"; the *Sturm und Drang* literary movement, of which Marx was a follower, sounded similar notes. Mind was not to be seen as passively and mechanically reflecting an "objective" world, but as actively and creatively entering into relation with what is outside itself. It was not just Romantic poets but idealist philosophers, such as Kant, Schiller, Fichte and Hegel, who were reacting against the atomistic, mechanistic, and calculating features of the Enlightenment. They stressed, instead, the autonomous, moral, and self-creating aspects of humans—Marx later noted that "Hegel conceives of the self-creation of man as a process"—and claimed the external world to be a field on which man might battle for, as well as express, his inner spiritual and even aesthetic nature.

Samuel Taylor Coleridge wrote of how "the philosophy of mechanism, which, in everything that is most worthy of the human intellect, strikes *Death*," and Keats exclaimed how "in these cold and enfeebling times . . . romance lives but in books . . . and the rainbow is robbed of its mystery." Marx, in the same vein (though at a time later in his career when he wrote, not poems, but about aesthetics), asked rhetorically:

Is the view of nature and of social relations which shaped Greek imagination and thus Greek mythology possible in the age of automatic machinery and railways and locomotives and electric telegraphs? Where does Vulcan come in as against Roberts and Co., Jupiter as against the lightning rod, and Hermes as against the Credit Mobilier? All mythology masters and dominates and shapes the forces of nature in and through imagination; hence it disappears as soon as man gains mastery over the forces of nature. What becomes of the Goddess Fame side by side with Printing House Square? Or is the Iliad at all possible in a time of the hand-operated or the later steam press? Are not singing and reciting and the muse necessarily put out of existence by the printer's bar; and do not necessary prerequisites of epic poetry accordingly vanish?[5]

Epic poetry, such as the *Iliad*, was no longer possible, at least in its old form. But Marx, I would argue, wrote another kind of epic poem in *Capital*—where his allusion to Dante's *Divine Comedy* suggests what he had in mind—and created a new mythology of enormous potency. We shall return to this subject in Chapter VIII.

III

In embracing the Romantic attitude, young Karl was joining his generation's questioning of the Enlightenment, its values, and its commercial underpinnings. Engels missed this point when he spoke of the strands that went into Marx's protean synthesis. Romantic anti-capitalist feelings entered into Marx's philosophic and revolutionary critique as much, for example, as English classical economic theory.

Marx, in embracing Romantic anti-capitalism, and rejecting Enlightenment values (except for the core belief in progress), was also challenging his father, a typical follower of the *philosophes*, and the older man, in response to his son's letters, did not hesitate to make his own views known. For him, the spate of high-flown romantic rhetoric represented the utterances of "new monsters." As he wrote his son, "You are following in the footsteps of the new monsters that mumble their words until they can no longer hear themselves speak; they have only confused ideas or none at all, and so a flood of words is described as the birth of a genius."

Satiric as it is, does the father's letter point out a part of Marx's being and "genius"? Reading Marx's texts, one is struck by the "flood of words," by the way effusive language is often substituted for careful analysis. Even his sympathetic headmaster at the gymnasium, Johann Hugo Wyttenbach, remarked of Marx's school essay that he "constantly seeks for elaborate picturesque expressions. . . . Therefore many passages . . . lack the necessary clarity."[6] The "old" Marx did not give up his youthful tricks. He seems intoxicated by the sound of certain words and turns of phrase. He is utterly enamored of chiastic phrases, where the order of syntactical elements is inverted: "The *social* emancipation of the Jew is the *emancipation of society from Judaism*"; or, "*Man makes religion; religion does not make man*"; or, playing on the title of Proudhon's book, *The Philosophy of Poverty*, Marx entitles his critique, *The Poverty of Philosophy*. Cleverness in inverting a phrase is not necessarily the same as overthrowing an idea, or society, but Marx often makes it sound as if it were.

After reading much of Marx's writings, especially some of the youthful manuscripts, there is the temptation to say of parts of it, "Sound and fury. . . ." Other parts, however, are, indeed, great "poetic" creations. The *Manifesto*, like *Capital*, is another of the great epics of all time. Its roots, though largely hidden, are in the style first manifested in the poems, the novel, and the drama of the romantic youth of 1837. Heinrich Marx was partly right: both a "new monster" and a "genius" were being born in the volume later dedicated to him in spite of his rejecting words.

Karl Marx's own favorite poets, he tells us later in his life, are Shakespeare, Aeschylus, and Goethe. He is clearly not in their company. The loss for literature becomes a gain for us in that, unlike a protean Shakespeare, masquerading in all the figures of his poetry, our young author is markedly and naïvely self-revelatory. This trait persists throughout his life. As a mature adult, playing the game of "Confessions" with his daughter Laura he gives us more clues to his nature. Asked about "his favourite virtue in man," he answered "Strength"; in woman, "Weakness." His "idea of happiness," "to fight"; of misery, "submission." "The vice you detest most," "Servility." These themes sound familiar. The mature man and the youthful poet are one.

When the defiant romantic becomes the father of scientific socialism, the style in which he does this is often as important as the content; indeed, the two, as in all good writing, are fused, and it is the fusion which explodes into our minds. So, too, it is the passion which imbues the sentences and not just their rational message which has the power to enthrall us. The style and the passion, along with the themes, are displayed in Marx's written work, but take their origin in his living, breathing person. The same person who wrote the great Marxist works wrote the awkward, adolescent poems we have been analyzing.

III

Religion
and the Call
to a Vocation

In 1835, young Karl, as a gymnasium student, wrote a final exam paper on an assigned religious topic, "The Union of Believers with Christ."[1] His teacher judged it "profound in thought, brilliantly and forcefully written, deserving of praise," though adding that part of the subject was dealt with "only one-sidedly." Anyone reading it today would come to a different conclusion. It is neither profound nor brilliant. It breathes of pious, supine, acceptable Christian doctrine. It also surprises anyone familiar with the assertive and later atheistic Marx.

In fact, knowledge of Marx's later virulent anti-religious feelings colors the attitude of most scholars to his earlier religious experiences. "How," they seem to be asking, "can he have ever been religious-minded, he who attacked religion so vehemently?" They point to his father and teachers, as rationalists and deists, whose views presumably weighed heavily on the young boy. Thus so eminent a scholar as Auguste Cornu dismisses the ostensibly Christian religious content as being "deistic" in the merely rationalist Enlightenment traditions.[2]

I think this attitude inaccurately imposes the burden of the past on the actual development of young Karl and thereby misses a point of great importance. It is essential to look at the materials—and Marx's text—with fresh eyes. Trier, Marx's birthplace, was itself a very religious town, marked by its cathedral and convents. Early 19th-century Prussia and its Rhineland possessions, especially in the reactionary period after Napoleon, were also wrapped in a pietistic religious atmosphere. Breaking free of this heritage was a task many young Germans faced. We must not underestimate their initial commitment by focusing only on their revolt. The Higher Criticism, i.e., the bringing of historical standards of judgment to the Old and New Testaments, was necessary for young Hegelians because, on a less lofty plane, they had been believers. Karl Marx, like many of his contemporaries, was imbued willy-nilly with the deeply Christian worldview of someone brought up in such an atmosphere, whatever his commitment to specific doctrines.

More specifically, however, even if young Karl does give, as we shall see, a "moral" slant to his essay—he is not a theologian—it is a distinctly Christian moral slant, with no evidence of disbelief in Christ's divinity or mission. In the text of his exam, he specifically quotes four passages from the New Testament (John 15) and makes much of the parable of the vine and the branches.

Was this out of prudence? Such a motive may have played a minor part in the composition, but it cannot explain the general reverential tone of the essay. The argument that Johann Hugo Wyttenbach, the head of the gymnasium, was a rationalist who must have influenced Marx cuts two ways: the young scholar, knowing his headmaster's views, need not have felt compelled to express a deferential Christianity. What about Karl's father, Heinrich? He had converted to Christianity, as we shall detail, but hardly as a religious believer. Though he was not one to challenge established authority openly, or to take violent offense at the mouthing of Christian platitudes, might not his luke-warm attitudes impose themselves on his son? This conclusion confuses the father with the son: unlike the adult Heinrich, who prudentially converted late in life, Karl was brought up as a Christian from the age of six.

At his graduation, young Karl was already exhibiting the defiance that marked him so strongly in later life. In spite of his father's cautionary admonitions to the contrary, the son refused to pay his respects at his school leaving to a reactionary co-headmaster appointed to balance the liberal Wyttenbach. Why was there not equal, if masked, defiance in the school essay, if he really was anti-Christian?

There can be no conclusive answer to this and other questions as to how sincere and deeply-rooted were Karl Marx's early religious beliefs—the evidence is simply not sufficient—and we must settle for the most persuasive findings. On balance, I believe that Marx was a believing

Christian in his early years, though obviously not a theological fanatic; to think otherwise is to dismiss or downgrade many of the themes that continue into his later writings.

I find additional support for my overall view in the scholarly investigations of Abraham Rotstein, who argues that the line of Western apocalyptic thought leads from Luther through Hegel to Marx.[3] Hegel openly affirmed, "I am a Lutheran and am . . . rooted in Lutheranism through philosophy. . . ." The concepts of lordship (*Herrschaft*) and bondage (*Knechtschaft*), which figure so prominently in Hegel's *Phenomenology of Spirit*, reach back to Luther and behind him to the Bible, and forward to Marx. Marx did not go as far as Hegel in proclaiming himself in later life a Lutheran, but in his "Contribution to the Critique of Hegel's *Philosophy of Right*" he acknowledged that "Germany's *revolutionary* past is theoretical—it is the Reformation." The rhetoric of inversion and transformation used by Marx mirrors that of Luther's usage, and Marx himself remarks that "in that period [the Reformation] the revolution originated in the brain of a monk, today in the brain of the philosopher."[4]

Marx was also influenced in his language by Luther's translation of the Bible, as well as by the Christian notion that out of nothing comes everything; that one must die to be reborn; and that the last shall be first. (As Luther wrote in "On the Bondage of the Will," the path for true believers is "that being humbled and brought back to nothingness by this means they may be saved"; Marx, later, wrote of the proletariat as that class "with radical chains . . . universal suffering . . . unqualified wrong . . . perpetrated on it" which will then be saved and inherit the earth.)[5]

Marx is squarely in the redemptive tradition: he writes of how the proletariat moves from its own "complete loss of humanity and can only redeem itself through the total redemption of humanity." Is that tradition Christian or Jewish? Some argue that Marx is heir of the tradition of the great Jewish prophets, thundering forth at mankind. Insofar as the Jewish tradition becomes part of the Christian, as it does in the Bible, I would agree (after all, Christ, too, was born a Jew). But Marx received that tradition, I am arguing, in its Lutheran form, as a result of being raised as a believing Christian. Marx, needless to say, did not remain a believing Christian (any more than Luther was a forerunner of communism). As Rotstein asserts, however, "What they do share in common is a rhetorical structure, namely the characteristic articulation of the apocalyptic tradition that moves step by step . . . from the original condition of domination and oppression to the culmination of perfect community." That rhetorical structure which Marx received in his Lutheran upbringing underlies his creation of a secular religion.

II

In his paper on "The Union of Believers with Christ," the young gymnast writes that in Christianity, "Virtue is no longer a dark distorted image, as it was depicted by the philosophy of the Stoics"; in his doctoral dissertation to come, 1840–41, he will praise the Stoics. Union with Christ, we are told, bestows "inner exultation, consolation," etc., "not out of ambition, not through a desire for fame, but only because of Christ"; the poem of 1835 as we have seen, preached another conviction. "Therefore union with Christ bestows a joy which the Epicurean strives vainly to derive from his frivolous philosophy"; the doctoral dissertation, on the "Difference Between the Democritean and Epicurean Philosophy of Nature," will use very different language and come to opposite conclusions.[6]

Was Marx a hypocrite, a question at which I have already hinted? Or was the young Karl merely confused and ambivalent? Or a true believer, unknowingly on the edge of losing his faith as I am suggesting? To help secure an answer to such queries, let us look now at Marx's religious background and beliefs.

Karl's parents, as is well known, were of Jewish background. Indeed, on both sides of the family a line of rabbinical ancestors stretched behind the young examinee. His father Heinrich, originally Hirschel, had been born a Jew, turned away from his religion in the name of Enlightenment ideals, and converted to Christianity (Lutheranism) in 1816 for prudential reasons. As a lawyer who had been the beneficiary of the civil liberties bestowed on Jews by the French Revolutionary and Napoleonic "liberation" of the Rhineland, it behooved him at the time of the conservative restoration of Prussian rule in 1815 at Napoleon's downfall to embrace the official religion, which would allow him to continue his practice. He seems to have suffered no pain in the convenient conversion.[7]

Six years later, in 1824, Heinrich had his children also baptized. A year later, his wife, Henriette, grudgingly followed suit. Heinrich's mother

had died the year before the children were baptized, and Henriette's father, just before she was baptized; it may have been out of filial respect,
therefore, that they waited as they did.

In any case, Karl grew up as a confirmed Lutheran. His mother, born
Pressburg, in Holland, of a family earlier from Hungary, seems not to
have been wholly accepting of the change; nevertheless, she acceded to
her husband's request. Indeed, it seems she was generally less adaptable,
never learning, for example, to write correct German, and earned a certain amount of scorn from her bright, ambitious child. Whatever real
training and catechism in the Christian religion he obtained was not
from his mother or his practical father, but in school.

The conversion of Jews to Christianity in the early 19th century was
something of a commonplace. As the Enlightenment brought them out
of the ghetto, Jews frequently turned to Christianity as a way into the
wider culture, while rejecting the clericalism that surrounded it. Heine
in Germany, Disraeli in England were famous Jewish Christians. Heinrich Marx, and his son, Karl, therefore, were not exceptional in their
religious experiences.

In Trier, the home city of the Marxes, almost all of the population
of around twelve to fifteen thousand were Catholics; only about five
hundred were Prostestant (and about 260 were Jewish).[8] But Prussia,
sovereign over the Rhineland, was Protestant—Lutheran, in fact. The
Marxes, in becoming Protestants rather than Catholics, were identifying
with the bureaucratic elite.

For Karl, Protestant Christianity was, I believe, an accepted part of
his early development. The evidence, as I have argued, suggests that,
in 1835, like most other Germans, he accepted the obligatory teachings
offered him without undue strain or scepticism. He appears to have been
a true believer, whose thoughts and feelings as a result were deeply steeped
in the Christian tradition, with religious attitudes a vital part of his early
personal life and outlook.

Now, it must be stated that, always eager to unmask others, Marx
could hide his own true feelings, as, when flattering and supporting
someone publicly, he would undercut him in private correspondence to
Engels. Yet, Wilhelm Liebknecht, who became one of the leaders of
the German social democrats, in his recollections wrote of Marx, "He
was as incapable as a child of wearing a mask or pretending . . . he
always spoke his mind completely and without any reserve and his face
was the mirror of his heart . . . Marx was never a hypocrite. He was

absolutely incapable of it, just like an unsophisticated child."[9] Lieb-knecht, a devoted disciple, was clearly naïve—and wrong. In principle, therefore, Marx was certainly capable of being a hypocrite.

The question, here, is whether as a young man he was in fact being hypocritical about his religious feelings. For example, in the poems, we have seen him wrestling with his mixed "feelings" and expressing sentiments of ambition that conflict with those in the religious essay. I hold to the position, nevertheless, that Marx was not hypocritical in this particular instance, but unable to bring his warring impulses into one focus. His Christian beliefs told him that ambition was sinful; his romantic strivings inspired him, "on the pulse," i.e., emotionally, to be ambitious. Always convinced of his rightness, egotistical, and ambitious, he expressed himself openly in these terms. It is one reason why we can come to know what I shall call the outer, or public, man so well. Marx was not introspective, seeking to know himself. Such self-examination for him was "brooding," to be rejected through or in favor of action. In spite of such a rejection, it is likely that he felt guilty in some inner part of his soul, but he did not allow himself to be either conscious or troubled on the surface of his life, by the obvious contradictions. It was a useful trait for a future Hegelian.

The poems and the Christian piety exist in separate worlds of meaning. Within a year or two, however, either just before going off to university or upon entrance, the young man lost his faith. To put it that way is, in fact, too weak. He became a militant atheist, a scoffer at the "union with Christ," a challenger of the Christian God as well as of the Promethean gods of his poems. The virulence of his reaction suggests the vehemence of his earlier beliefs: one rarely rejects something violently about which one has never had strong feelings. We have no documentation, however, for the cause of his loss of faith, or its vicissitudes.

Behind his repudiated Christianity now appeared his Judaism. One of his first writings was to be "On the Jewish Question." Religion, in the sense I have been discussing it, Protestant or Jewish, was of central importance to Karl Marx's life and thought. The powerful attraction of Hegel would be partly because he dealt with the religious question centrally: Hegel himself had started as a theological student and then shifted to a philosophy that was a form of religion transcended. Marx honored Hegel, and in the "Contribution to the Critique of Hegel's *Philosophy of Right"* (1844), began by saying, "The criticism of religion is the premise of all criticism."

As we shall see, Marx, following upon Hegel and Feuerbach, believed that religion was the creation of man, which then claimed to have created him and consequently to command him, i.e., man had erected the very gods in whose name he then bowed down. (Marx would apply the same analysis to capitalist economics.) In thinking in these religious (actually, anti-religious) terms, Marx impresses us as a young man who feels he has been taken in, and now must destroy the false authority that has misled him in his innocent youth.

III

At the time that Karl wrote the religious exam essay, he was obliged to write another examination question that was of his own choice. He chose the topic, "Reflection of a Young Man on the Choice of a Profession."[10] The sentiments expressed in this essay confirm our view that Marx was not being hypocritical about his religious beliefs. They also offer us further insights into the struggle going on within his youthful soul.

He begins by drawing a distinction between man and the animals: the latter have their sphere of activity determined for them and have no idea of anything beyond it. To man, however "the Deity gave a general aim, that of ennobling mankind and himself." How man goes about doing this, however, is a matter of choice. At this point a note of anxiety enters Karl's essay: "This choice is a great privilege of man over the rest of creation, but at the same time it is an act which can destroy his whole life, frustrate all his plans, and make him unhappy." These are strong, indeed hyperbolic, terms.

God's voice, fortunately, will guide man in his choice. "This voice can easily be drowned," however, and we be misled by false inspiration. We must examine "whether this inspiration is a delusion, and what we took to be a call from the Deity was self-deception." Then follows a disturbing and revealing statement: "What is great glitters, its glitter arouses ambition, and ambition can easily have produced the inspiration, or what we took for inspiration; but reason can no longer restrain the man who is tempted by the demon of ambition, and he plunges headlong into what impetuous instinct suggests. . . . " So tempted, we shall end up "inveigh[ing] against the Deity and curse mankind." Here Karl has cast his inner strife in typically Christian terms: is it the voice of God or the Devil that is driving him onward?

God's voice may be inauthentic, and our own reason an untrustworthy guide. To what or whom then can we turn? Our parents, Karl answers, who have lived and experienced the vicissitudes of life. Following their advice, we may grasp our true vocation.

Even then the problem is not resolved, for "we cannot always attain the position to which we are called; our relations in society have to some extent already begun to be established before we are in a position to determine them." What does the young student have in mind? Is he thinking of his own position as a bourgeois in a stratified society? Or is he thinking of himself as a converted Jew, with all the bars that might place around him?

In any event, the personal observation later finds its echo in ideology. In a prosaic article on economic distress and freedom of the press written for the *Rheinische Zeitung* in 1843, Marx wrote, "In the investigation of *political* conditions one is too easily tempted to overlook *the objective nature of the relationships* and to explain everything from the *will* of the persons acting. There are *relationships*, however, which determine the actions of private persons as well as those of individual authorities, and which are as independent as are the movements in breathing."[11] If this appears arcane, Marx put the matter more directly in "The Eighteenth Brumaire of Louis Bonaparte" (1852), when he remarked that "Men make their own history; but . . . not . . . under conditions of their own choosing."[12] The mature Marx thus once again comments on the gap between individual will and circumscribing relations or conditions, and between personal experience and ideological expression.

Among these conditions, Marx gives special and immediate attention to the "physical constitution" which "is often a threatening obstacle, and let no one scoff at its rights." If one cannot rise above this obstacle, then one's "whole life is an unhappy struggle between the mental and the bodily principle." Did the young man have a premonition of the bodily ills that would plague his later life—the headaches and carbuncles—whose aspects now seem to us psychosomatic? We know that his parents, and especially his mother, fretted about his health, over-cautioning him about risks to his physical constitution. In later life Marx appeared to have fulfilled his parents' warnings with a vengeance: an odd form of being a dutiful son while rebelling against the parental injunctions. The hint to this effect comes in the next paragraph, when he indicates his compulsion: "The thought nevertheless continually arises of sacrificing our well-being to duty, of acting vigorously although we are weak."

Ill-health, then, though a threat (and a promise), cannot keep us from fulfilling our vocation. But lack of talent can. The thought of not carrying out successfully our vocation awakens strong and threatening feelings in Marx. The consequence of such failure, he writes, is self-contempt, and he goes on, "What feeling is more painful and less capable of being made up for by all that the outside world has to offer?" He continues, "Self-contempt is a serpent that ever gnaws at one's breast, sucking the life-blood from one's heart and mixing it with the poison of misanthropy and despair."

Where had the seventeen-year-old boy learned about self-contempt? Is anxiety the other side of ambition? If egotism and self-love are at one end of a spectrum of narcissism, are self-contempt and loathing at the other end? Somewhere in his native constitution or in the conditions of his life, Karl Marx had explored the borderline between the two extremes, feared the fall into self-contempt and despair, and pulled himself away from the edge toward creativity.[13]

The means of salvation lay in choosing a worthy vocation. It should be the one "which offers us the widest scope to work for mankind" and beckons to us with the prospect of achieving "perfection." Young Karl does not even pause to consider the illusion or danger involved in aiming at perfection. The ideal of striving for perfection was a religious truism, which, secularized, became the Enlightenment idea of progress. Instead, he goes on to assert that worth can be assured and measured only by a profession "in which we are not servile tools." The confession of the old man whose most detested vice is servility is again prefigured in the young boy. Once more we must bear in mind the question as to why and where servility became a threat to Karl Marx.*

The professions which hold the greatest danger for Karl are those concerned with abstract truths instead of being involved with life itself. His principles may not yet be firm enough; yet he will be capable of

---

*Was it in the episode, possibly apocryphal, in which his father, Heinrich, reportedly abased himself before the Prussian authorities when reprimanded about his participation in a "radical" banquet (at which the "Marseillaise" was sung)? Karl Marx was then sixteen; whatever grains of truth are in the story may have caused him to look upon his father as a man with clay feet, or at least as unheroic.

sacrificing his life for these possibly false principles. Shaking off these vague and troubling thoughts, the author affirms that the chief guide to a choice of professions "is the welfare of mankind and our own perfection." The latent conflict between the general good and self-glorification is dealt with promptly: "It should not be thought that these two interests would be in conflict . . . on the contrary, man's nature is so constituted that he can attain his own perfection only by working for the perfection, for the good of his fellow men."

One model is Jesus Christ. "Religion itself," Karl notes, "teaches us that the ideal being whom all strive to copy sacrificed himself for the sake of mankind." (Incidentally, this sentiment is hardly requisite, even for a hypocritical Marx, in an essay on choosing a profession.) History confirms religion's instruction and speaks of other noble servants of mankind. Karl's optimistic conclusion is that if, like these beings, we choose a profession that most benefits mankind, "we shall experience no petty, limited, selfish joy, but our happiness will belong to millions, our deeds will live on quietly but perpetually at work, and over our ashes will be shed the hot tears of noble people."

In spite of the sanguine conclusion, we sense a troubled, uncertain young man. He is wrestling with acute problems of self-esteen. He is worried about body and mind. He has in mind the loftiest ideal—perfection in the service of mankind—but fears that he may be being misled by some evil spirit, a demon. He cannot avoid a choice—one that is constrained by conditions as well as doubt. In the first instance, the choice must be one of vocation. In the poems, he has already made his choice of love: Jenny; in the school essays, he is still thrashing about as to the choice of work. Young Karl is clearly a youth in turmoil and strife. His choice of career, as we know, will implicate the world in a good deal of turmoil and strife as well.

IV

Father and Son,
and the Ghost of Hegel

Under the injunctions of his father—the guide spoken of in the school essay—Karl initially chose jurisprudence as his vocation. Heinrich Marx was a successful lawyer; he wished Karl to be even more successful. What was more natural than that the son should enroll at the University of Bonn as a law student?

Karl's leaving certificate from the gymnasium in Trier spoke of him as "of evangelical faith" and stated that his "moral behaviour towards superiors and fellow pupils was good."[1] He is noted as being well-grounded in knowledge of the Christian faith and morals, with some acquaintance with the history of the church. His aptitude and diligence in ancient languages and German were very satisfactory, though, oddly enough, he is marked down as not trying very hard in French. In fact, Marx was extremely gifted at languages and was able to write fluently in French, and eventually, English, as well as, of course, German. In physics, his knowledge was judged "moderate." All in all, his teachers had "favorable expectations," for their bright, well-behaved pupil, off to study jurisprudence.

Within a year or so, he had changed course. His new vocation was to be philosophy. We are fortunate in having the one surviving letter from Karl to his father deal at length and in depth with this turning point in his life. It is written from Berlin, where he had gone after a somewhat bilious and even frivolous year as a student at Bonn.

Karl was fully conscious and even proud of the transformation being wrought. "There are moments in one's life," he writes, "which are like frontier posts marking the completion of a period but at the same time clearly indicating a new direction."[2] With a certain egotism, Karl adds, "Indeed, world history itself likes to look back in this way and take stock . . ." Such phrasing makes it clear that he has been reading Hegel, as he will confess a little later on in the letter.

What is also clear is that Karl saw his life in Hegelian developmental terms. Contradiction is essential, for only so does development occur. Karl's own life is, like world history, dialectical; that is its logic. I must confess that Marx's view of his life as a microcosm of the "logic" of history impresses me as a piece of *hubris*. It is essential, however, to realize that for Marx, psychology is actually philosophy, i.e., the Hegelian dialectic. Whatever view he had of his inner struggles was in these "logical" terms. *

Karl next compares the metamorphosis in his life to the writing of a new poem. His life, therefore, is an artistic creation as well as a dialectic development. The poetry is connected to Jenny and love (as we saw when I discussed his poems in Chapter II), and Karl tells his father how the new world of love came into existence for him. Yet, looking at the poems objectively, he is aware that they are marked by a "complete opposition between what is and what ought to be." What they express is merely "a longing that has no bounds."

In the "Reflections," we recall that Karl had said that a young man's true guides were his parents. The same note persists in the letter to his

---

* Immanuel Kant believed that "passions are cancers for pure practicable reason and often incurable"; he would have liked to do away with passions and replace them with reason. Friedrich Schiller rejected Kant's fragmentation of man's nature, and wished to see man whole, i.e., motivated by passions and reason together. Georg Wilhelm Friedrich Hegel, building on Schiller's suggestions, conceived of man's psychological development in dialectical terms, as "sublimating" *(aufhebend)* past passions and reason into a present moment: as he writes in *The Phenomenology of Spirit*, "The individual must also pass through the contents of the educational stages of the general spirit." It is within this "psychological" tradition that Marx needs to be placed. (For a useful treatment of this subject, see *Hegel: Reinterpretation, Texts, and Commentary*, by Walter Kaufmann [Garden City, N.Y. 1965]). What Marx will add is a new stress on man's physical labor in the world, as a means of realizing, or creating, his nature. Even more importantly, Marx will then analyze this "labor" in terms of the economic conditions of production, i.e., the "materialist" interpretation of history. While this is an enormously important development in its own terms—Marx's true achievement—its underpinnings in idealistic "psychology" must still be recognized, with all the limitations (along with the insights) attendant thereon.

father, where he compares a parent's heart to a "sacred dwelling place." Karl has a problem. He must tell his father that he is abandoning the law for philosophy, turning from a potentially profitable and honorable pursuit to a chancy profession of thought. He goes about stating all this very delicately.

Poetry, he says, is only a diversion. He has to study law and, he adds, wrestle with philosophy, for the two are really closely linked. At this point, he snows the reader, if not his father. He makes learned references to Heineccius and Thibaut, to the Pandect and Roman law, and outlines a plan for the philosophical treatment of law. He describes the plan in the letter—the work itself of almost three hundred pages was discarded—observing that the prime defect in it was the characteristic vice of idealism, i.e., the opposition between what is and what ought to be.

Karl informs his father that he then turned from this arid exercise back to "the dances of the Muses." The resulting compositions of *Scorpion and Felix* and *Oulanem* (which I mentioned earlier) are sent to Heinrich in an exercise book. Karl believes that in these works he glimpsed the nature of true poetry, but in the end was "not much enriched." Moreover, he had paid a heavy price: sleepless nights and much internal and external excitement. His body weakened and a doctor advised him to go to the country to recuperate, he writes. His parents' warnings had come true.

In the country, Karl claims that he matured "from an anemic weakling into a man of robust bodily strength." With the physical change comes an abrupt mental transformation. The next sentence tells Karl's father that "A curtain had fallen, my holy of holies was rent asunder, and new gods had to be installed." The imagery is religious; the implicit psychology involved has to do with the fall of God the Father, and perhaps another father as well. Heinrich's deism is being displaced by Karl's atheism. The substance is philosophical; in moving from Kant to Hegel, Karl is going beyond his father's Enlightenment views.

Hegel would lead Marx from idealism per se to finding the idea in reality itself. Karl tells his father that he had written a twenty-four-page dialogue in which he had given "a philosophical-dialectical account of divinity, as it manifests itself in the idea-in-itself, as religion, as nature, and as history. My last proposition was the beginning of the Hegelian system."

Inspired by Hegel, Marx was yet ambivalent about his mentor. The

letter in which he tells about his feelings is itself confusing. He felt Hegel was a "false siren," an "idol" whose view he "hated" (in the school
essays, the young Marx's fear of being misled has already been sounded
as a pervasive major theme). Upset over his hateful attachment, worried
about Jenny, sleepless, he became ill. While ill, he read Hegel, as he
says, "from beginning to end," got to know his disciples and joined a
Doctors' Club composed of young Hegelians. Karl had become infected
with the Hegelian virus sweeping Germany.

The involvement with the Doctors' Club meant an affiliation with
the left-wing Hegelians, and especially with Bruno Bauer. Karl was not
only turning to philosophy, but to radical philosophy, and thus radical-
ism. Of course, he does not spell this out to his father. Instead, he moves
on to a muddled account of his feelings, all leading to his second prime
motive for writing the letter: he wants his father's permission to return
home to visit Jenny.

He coats the request by describing how he has made the acquaintance of an assessor, who has given him valuable advice as to succeeding
in the legal profession. He alludes to his mother's illness, his brother's
condition, and his desire to see them, and adds, "But, my dear, very
good father, would it not be possible to discuss all this with you personally?" Aware that his father may see through his pretentions, he lamely
goes on, "Believe me, my dear, dear father, I am actuated by no selfish
intention (although it would be bliss for me to see Jenny again)."

Then, in heavy, sentimental language, he asks his father to forgive
his erring, agitated state, and to believe in his heartfelt love. In a postscript, he adds an additional request for forgiveness: "It is almost 4 o'clock,
the candle has burnt itself out, and my eyes are dim; a real unrest has
taken possession of me, I shall not be able to calm the turbulent spectres
until I am with you who are dear to me."

Any parent with a child at school may recognize much that is familiar in a letter such as the one Karl wrote his father. Any young college
student may blush a bit over similar ones he or she has written. Karl's
is probably more romantic and sentimental than the average; he was undoubtedly influenced by the prevailing style of his time. It is also likely
that his letter is more pretentious than most. It is certain that it is more
portentous. Anyone who has read *The Communist Manifesto*, with
its reference to the "spectre"—Communism—"haunting Europe," will
be prepared to consider whether, in exorcising his own "turbulent

spectres," young Karl, as the rest of this book will attempt to show, has projected them in an extraordinary sense onto the world at large.

II

We have heard from Karl. What about Heinrich, his father, the other voice in this dialogue? We are lucky; although only one letter from Karl survives, a goodly number survive from his father.[3] In fact, we even have the letter to which Karl was responding on November 10 (11), 1837. This letter of Heinrich's is best read as part of a series, but we will cite it first.

It was written approximately on 20 August 1837 (Karl was, as always, dilatory in replying to his parent). The socially ambitious Heinrich begins by informing his son that a tutor to the son of a Prince will look him up, and may be helpful in the approaching vacation. Then Heinrich moves on to the question of Karl's going to Berlin: he recognizes that Berlin has advantages over Bonn, but laments that the former city is distant, and that parental desires "would be largely shattered by your residing so far away." "Of course," Heinrich hastens to add, "that must not hinder your plan of life; parental love is probably the least selfish of all." *But*, he goes on, *if* Karl could combine his plans with his parents' desires, this would bring him joy, "the number of which decreases so considerably with the years."

This is the letter to which Karl was responding. It contains a number of messages that are mainly contradictory. The father wants Karl to be ambitious, and to further himself. But not if this means removing himself from his parents. He doesn't want Karl to alter his plans; but, of course, he does want him to. Underlying the contradictions is the assertion that parents, by definition, are unselfish; if Karl acts against their wishes, he is obviously selfish. Hanging over the letter as a whole is the sense that his father is declining in joys, and that Karl is his last source of such satisfactions. In short, the letter puts the son in the classic double bind. Ironically, such doublethink also coincides in part with, and perhaps prepares him for, the use of dialectical logic.

Earlier and later letters make this conclusion ever more evident. In the very first letter (November 8, 1835) we have from Heinrich to his son, the carping, accusing note (however justified) is struck reverberatingly: "More than three weeks have passed since you went away, and there is no sign of you! You know your mother and how anxious she is, and yet you show this boundless negligence." Heinrich then enlarges the specific complaint into a general character analysis: "That, unfortunately, only too strongly confirms the opinion, which I hold in spite of your many good qualities, that in your heart *egoism* is predominant (italics mine)."

The father hides his anxiety behind the mother—"For my part, I can wait," he writes. We are not convinced. Karl, too, would feel the insincerity in his father's letter. Much worse is the accusation of egoism. We can guess that this is not the first time it has been made. What makes it worse is that it comes from an obviously loving parent. The accusation will haunt Karl throughout his life.

In his early years, as we have been seeing, Marx is wrestling with the question of personal, and thus selfish, ambition, in contrast to unselfish service to mankind. Rhetorically, he opts for a vocation that will serve humanity; in the same breath, however, he wondered whether he is being misled by a demon—and therefore fooling himself. His most savage attacks, in his chosen vocation as a radical reformer, will be, as we shall see, on the self-interest—egoism—defended and even glorified by the classical economists. Adam Smith's revolution had been in these terms; while he approved of benevolence as a moral philosopher, he accepted and analyzed the role of self-interest as an economist. Karl Marx's counterrevolution would be to repudiate self-interest as a motive or mechanism that could drive the economic machine.

In 1835, however, he had to come to terms with his father's accusation of egoism and his father's ambivalences, as well as his own. In the very next letter (November 18, 1835), Heinrich apologizes for "pedantically" insisting on Karl's writing, and explains his heavy investment in his son's future: "You make up for what I in less favourable circumstances . . . could not achieve. I should like to see in you what perhaps I could have become, if I had come into the world with equally favourable prospects."

As if this confession that he is living his life again in his son is not enough, Henrich then goes on to suggest a reversal of roles: "You can fulfill or destroy my best hopes. It is perhaps both unfair and unwise to build one's best hopes on someone and so perhaps undermine one's own tranquility. But who else than nature is to blame if men who are otherwise not so weak are nevertheless weak fathers?" Fathers are supposed to be strong. Is Heinrich strong or weak? His maudlin letter might well leave his beloved son in a quandary.

At the end of this letter, as of so many others to Karl, Heinrich warns him to take care of his health: "A sickly scholar is the most unfortunate being on earth. Therefore, do not study more than your health can bear." His mother's postscript to this letter emphasizes the point: "Allow me to note, dear Carl, that you must never regard cleanliness and order as something secondary, for health and cheerfulness depend on them. Insist strictly that your rooms are scrubbed frequently and fix a definite time for it—and you, my dear Carl, have a weekly scrub with sponge and soap." The response of the eighteen-year-old boy, as well as the mature man to be, to his parents' loving intrusion was to abuse his health and to lead a slovenly existence. So much for parental admonitions! To guard his independence and autonomy, the young Karl seems to have had to defy his parents' advice.

Money, too, was an area of special concern. Here, as well, his father vacillated. At one moment, he admonishes his son not to worry about finances; at another, he reminds him how extravagant he has been, and how little money, he, Heinrich, really has. We catch the flavor of this double bind with a few quotations. In early 1836, the father writes, "I enclose a money order for 50 talers, and on this occasion can only say that your only concern should be your studies and, without using more than is necessary, you should save yourself any further anxiety"; then he adds, "You haven't eked out your existence by cadging, I hope." A month or so later, in March, he writes, "You know quite well I am not rich," and accuses Karl of having "somewhat overstepped the bounds." Within a year, with Karl now at Berlin, the father's tone grows increasingly satirical and accusatory: "Only one thing more my Herr Son will still allow me, namely to express my surprise that I have still not received any request for money!" And again, "Only on one point . . . you have very wisely found fit to observe an aristocratic silence; I am referring to the paltry matter of money."

It is not surprising that money became a troubling subject for Marx. Throughout his personal life, he continued the pattern of taking from others, notably Engels, and spending it freely. The father's gibe about his son's aristocratic attitude was not off the mark. The small inheritance Marx got from his father, and then mother, were in a sense squandered. The personal solution to the double bind was to spend freely—as if it were necessary to get rid of a distasteful object—while yet remaining anxious about it—Marx is constantly writing about his money problems. The public solution was to excoriate money: in the *Economic and Philosophical Manuscripts*, he later refers to money as "The *pander* between . . . human life and the means of subsistence" and "the universal whore"—and calls for a society in which money is non-existent. Needless to say, it is money that stands at the core of capitalist economics.

Karl's inheritance from his father, however, included not only attitudes to money but the very idealism that eventually dictated the young man's solution to the problem. Heinrich, for example, writes of his son's "strict principles" with mixed feelings, adding that "these principles remind me of my bygone youth, and the more so since they were all I possessed." Later he comments, "Despite my grey hairs, somewhat depressed state of mind and all too many cares, I would still be defiant and despise what is base." Similarly, while ambitious and realistic, he boasts that "a practical man though I am, I have not been ground down to such a degree as to be blunted to what is high and good." When he adds, "Nevertheless, I do not readily allow myself to be completely torn up from the earth, which is my solid basis, and wafted exclusively into airy spheres where I have no firm ground under my feet," we seem to hear an anticipation of Marx's later transformation of idealism into materialism.[4]

Health, money, career—these are the double binds fettered about the young Karl by his well-intentioned father.[5] Or, as one of my students phrased it, "Jewish guilt." The heaviest incubus inherited by the young man was his father's "sad forebodings" that his son was "not free from a little more egoism than is necessary for self-preservation."[6] Karl was to spend the rest of his life sacrificing self, wife and children, in a material sense, to disprove his father's charge of egoism. In the end, however, we are not sure how to answer the father's question as to his son's genius: "Is that demon heavenly or Faustian?" As Nietzsche remarked, altruism can be the most refined form of egoism. Remaking the world in his own "altruistic" image may have been Karl Marx's way of serving both mankind and his own most intense narcissistic needs at one and the same time.

What we can be sure of is that young Karl Marx wrestled mightily with the question of his correct vocation and did so in terms and ways greatly influenced by his father. The latter's contradictory admonitions are a shadow over the later dialectical solutions worked out by the mature thinker, Marx. As the father himself summed it up for his son, in unintended Hegelian language, "You became estranged [alienated] from your family."[7] Even if we cannot spell out the exact details, we gain a deeper understanding of how the "father" of "scientific socialism" was very much the alienated son of his own earthly father, Heinrich.

V

Promethean Revolutionary or Dictator?

In an oft-repeated statement, Sigmund Freud remarked that the contented life was made up of Love and Work ("lieben und arbeiten," i.e., loving and working).[1] In winning Jenny, Karl Marx secured the loving part of his life in a firm and lasting manner. She represented his first real success in life. She was, in fact, a real "catch": beautiful, talented, of good family. As Marx wrote to her reminiscently in 1863, during a visit to Trier on the occasion of his mother's death, "I am asked daily on all sides about the former 'most beautiful girl in Trier' and 'Queen of the ball.' It is damned pleasant for a man when his wife lives on in the imagination of a whole city as a delightful princess."[2]

Marx, the communist, was proud of his wife's aristocratic lineage, and had her use on her calling card the words "neé von Westphalen." He valued her as a helpmate—she wrote out his manuscripts in a fair hand, and aided his work in innumerable other ways. He esteemed her as the mother of his children and caretaker of his household, in circumstances of poverty to which she was unaccustomed. Above all, he seems truly to have loved her, and she him—a love that shines through their Victorian, semi-exploitive and sexist marriage. Marx wrote to her, "But love—not of Feuerbachian man, not of Moleschott's metabolisms, not of the proletariat, but love of one's darling, namely you, makes a man into a man again."[3]

At its base the relationship was one of human love, of the kind which Marx was to extol in his *Economic and Philosophic Manuscripts*, though it was not untroubled and untested. Marx could be, as he put it, of "a hard nature." Jenny could be, and was, nervous and "mercurical." In the terrible period around 1850, marked by the death of their first child, Marx wrote to Engels about his wife's "floods of tears the whole night long" which "tire my patience and make me angry . . . I feel pity for my wife."[4] To escape, he fled to the British Museum.

Marx apparently also sought consolation with "another woman," at least briefly. Helene Demuth, the Marxes' servant and, more than servant, lynchpin of the house, was Jenny's helper from early days in Trier. It was "Lenchen," as she was called, who kept the household together, who made do on the little money they had, and who kept the family tempers on an even keel. In early 1851, she gave birth to an illegitimate son.

The father was Karl Marx, although his paternity was kept secret at the time and only made public by the chance discovery of a letter recently. Engels, in fact, on his deathbed, had told Karl's daughter, Eleanor; indeed, Engels had accepted paternity of the boy, known as "Freddy," to cover up for Marx. As for the true father, Marx, he never acknowledged the child as his own, and treated him badly. Whether out of fear of Jenny's jealousy, or of shame, or the use his enemies might make of the affair, Marx had nothing to do with the boy, who was not allowed to visit his mother while Marx lived (he was boarded out with a poor family, Engels picking up the tab), and who had to suffer an education restricted to the training accorded a future working man.[5]

What does this episode say of Marx? Can he, who attacked bourgeois sexual behavior in marriage as a form of legalized prostitution, and sex outside of marriage as exploitation of poor women who are forced into prostitution, be accused of hypocrisy? Does his personal behavior affect our judgment about his doctrines, and should it? These are questions to be dealt with elsewhere. Here we need only tell the story, and place it in its proper context. Marx dearly loved his wife; the illegitimate liaison with Lenchen was, I believe, a temporary straying, not affecting the central relationship.* On the whole, Marx was extraordinarily lucky in this vi-

---

* My friend Ralph Buultjens thinks otherwise. He believes Marx's virility and the close proximity to Lenchen would have made for a continuing affair. In his forthcoming book, *The Deadly Sin of Karl Marx*, Buultjens also cites the evidence for Marx having had two

tal area of his being. Jenny's love, and his love for her, provided the core of his emotional life, from which he could then seek his true vocation, confronting all its hazards boldly and confidently.

II

Secure in his affective life, Marx could turn his great energies outward to the world around him. He became a prodigious worker, although it was not clear to him what form other than rebellion his work should take, i.e., he had trouble choosing a career. We may note, too, that the world of work and workers became his central concern, although, unlike Engels, he knew little about actual factory work. Work in Marx's time had become industrial work, and it was Marx who became the leading philosopher of the Industrial Revolution, and the new society, and man, it was producing.

He began his own career, as we have seen, as a university student, first aiming at a profession of law and later aiming at a professorship of philosophy; he would next become a journalist and polemicist; and then shake down into the ill-defined life of a revolutionary, who spent more of his time in the British Museum than on the barricades. In fact, Marx never shed any of his vocational efforts except perhaps the legal: he remained a "professor" of philosophy manqué, "teaching" the workers; he continued writing journalistic articles throughout his life; and his revolution was as much in philosophy as in political life.

We have noted how young Karl's shift from an intention of being a lawyer to an interest in being a philosopher was intimately involved with his relations to his father. In moving from Kant to Hegel, from law per se to philosophy, he had, as his father recognized, gone beyond his parent. In actually going on to write his doctoral dissertation, he appears to have felt himself under the protection and encouragement of a second father, Ludwig von Westphalen.

The Baron was not just a father-in-law, but a powerful father-figure.

---

other known extra-marital "romances," one with his cousin Antoinette Philips. Buultjens concludes that it is not known whether that romance was consummated. In my view, the close proximity to Lenchen would be exactly what would make it too dangerous for Marx to continue with the affair. Another pregnancy—and contraceptives were unreliable at the time—or an accidental discovery would have shattered Marx's domestic life and destroyed the real affection existing between him and Jenny.

He was the father that Marx, in his romantic moments, wished to have. It was von Westphalen, at age sixty, who took long walks with the eighteen-year-old Karl, and talked of Homer and Shakespeare, rather than of Voltaire and Kant, the typical figures of Heinrich's Enlightenment; who encouraged Karl on one side to explore the romantic movement and on the other the incipient socialism of Saint-Simon. Though other members of the von Westphalen family opposed Karl's marriage to Jenny, for snobbish reasons, the Baron estimated his true intellectual worth, and gave his approval.

Karl returned the feelings redoubled. In 1841, three years after the death of his own father, he dedicated his doctoral dissertation to von Westphalen in lyrical terms.[6] He addressed him as "dear fatherly friend" and dedicated "these lines as a token of filial love." He spoke of von Westphalen as one whose idealism was sincere, and not merely rhetorical—a comment that can be read as a slap at Karl's real father—and who was always open to new ideas. Von Westphalen was, in short, the father we would all want. With his paternal blessing, even if Heinrich's was missing, Karl could go forward in good conscience.

The dissertation itself is on the "Difference between the Democritean and Epicurean Philosophy of Nature." It is a difficult, scholarly work, of little subsequent interest except that Marx wrote it. Marx argued that the epigoni of Hegel should be viewed as were the epigoni of Aristotle in antiquity, remaking the world itself philosophically after the great thinker had remade it merely in thought. In other words, Marx's real interest in the early Greek thinkers was due to his conviction that they were analogous to him and his contemporaries: they anticipated the way in which the neo-Hegelians might transform the real world in the image of Hegel. In Marx's words, "The result is that as the world becomes philosophical, philosophy also becomes worldly."[7]

There are two images in the dissertation which catch our attention. One is contained in a second analogy Marx draws between the way that philosophy develops and the way that an individual life, especially his own, unfolds. He writes, "As in the history of philosophy there are nodal points which raise philosophy in itself to concretion, apprehend abstract principles in a totality and thus break off the rectilinear process. . . ."[8] We have heard the language of "nodal points" before in Karl's letter to his father describing the nodal point in his own development. In short, Karl Marx's ontogeny recapitulates philosophy's phylogeny.

The other image involves Prometheus.[9] It is one of the most important and recurring images in Marx's work. It is clearly a self-image. It appears also to be connected with young Karl's view of his second father, with whom he is identifying: in the dedication, he speaks of von Westphalen as one who "with godly energy and manly confident gaze saw through all veils the empyreum which burns at the heart of the world."

Immediately following is the Foreword, in which Marx describes philosophy as "world-subduing," and informs us that "the confession of Prometheus: 'In simple words, I hate the pack of gods (Aesychylus, *Prometheus Bound*)', is its [philosophy's] own confession. . . ." To those who rejoice over philosophy's apparent fallen state in Prussia, Marx has philosophy—with himself as spokesman—respond "as Prometheus replied to the servant of the gods, Hermes":

> Be sure of this, I would not change my state
> Of evil fortune for your servitude.
> Better to be the servant of this rock
> Than to be faithful boy to Father Zeus.

Marx then concludes the Foreword, "Prometheus is the most eminent saint and martyr in the philosophical calendar."

III

A drawing of 1843 depicts Marx as Prometheus, tied to a printing press, a Prussian eagle pecking at his liver.[10] It was drawn on the occasion of the suppression of the *Rheinische Zeitung*, a periodical, as we shall see, of which Marx was then editor. At that time, having abandoned his career as a university philosopher and become a journalist, he still impressed his contemporaries as a Promethean figure, defying the gods of earth as well as heaven.

By affiliating with Bruno Bauer and the left Hegelians, Marx effectively ended his chances of obtaining a university post in philosophy. History can be affected by small events: if the Prussian government had allowed him to go into an academic career, would his bolts of lightning have safely gone into the ground of scholarly thought? Would the young radical have become the established professor, as so many since him have done? We will never know, for the opportunity was closed off to him at the very beginning of his academic vocation.

Marx turned his talents, instead, to journalism. By journalist, we do not mean a reporter, as on today's newspapers. A journalist then was connected with journals, or periodicals, and was closely related to what now we would describe as a columnist or editorial writer. In fact, many of Marx's pieces were extended essays on such subjects as the "Prussian Censorship Instruction," "Freedom of the Press," and "The Law on Thefts of Wood."

It was in mid-1842 that Marx began his work as a journalist, starting with an article that he sent to Arnold Ruge, the editor of the *Deutsche Jahrbücher*. In his new career, Marx hoped to earn a living, as well as to carry on his philosophical attack on authority. The article was the one on the censorship, referred to above; and it was, in fact, censored by the Prussian authorities, and thus never published as intended; it only appeared in print in 1843, as part of a book, *Anekdota*, edited by Ruge, and printed in Switzerland.

If the article offended Prussian officials, it appealed to a group of Rhenish businessmen who had put up money for the publication of the *Rheinische Zeitung*. Their main aims were practical: to agitate for the development of industry and commerce, and specifically for such acts as an expanded railway system and customs union. As liberal financiers and industrialists, they also favored a freer press and other democratic measures. Marx, moving from Bonn to Cologne, associated himself with the paper, and began to write for it. Within a short time, he became editor-in-chief.

Under Marx's powerful direction, the paper's circulation more than doubled. It began to be read throughout Prussia. Social and economic questions, as well as political ones, were arousing more and more interest in the 1840s as incipient industrialism came to Germany, as it had to England seventy to eighty years earlier. Socialist and communist solutions—the two terms were roughly interchangeable at the time—were much talked about in advanced circles. Marx, however, came slowly to this aspect of the contemporary situation. His philosophy hitherto had dreamed only of religious and political matters. Then in late 1842, he wrote an article on the theft of wood, in which he defended the customary rights of the peasants to the gathering of dead wood against the growing needs of industry to secure the timber by law.

In the article, Marx was still mainly concerned with the legal and political aspect. The question of private property, however, was central to his argument; it was one with which he would become more and more concerned. He was reaching another nodal point in his development. Later he wrote of this period, "In the year 1842–3, as Editor of the *Rheinische Zeitung*, I experienced for the first time the embarrassment of having to take part in discussions on the so-called material interests. The proceedings of the Rhineland Parliament on thefts of wood, and so on . . . provided the first occasion for occupying myself with the economic questions."

The censor was not going to let Marx occupy himself with these questions in the *Rheinische Zeitung*. Although he cleverly played games with the censor, Marx grew increasingly annoyed at his situation, and the government with him. Finally, in March 1843, Marx resigned in the face of an official decision to close down the paper. He may also have been pushed by the shareholders in the paper, who possibly hoped to save it by sacrificing him. In any case, Marx claimed to have felt liberated. His vocation lay elsewhere: in other countries and in other fields. In Germany, he wrote, "I can do nothing more. . . . Here one makes a counterfeit of oneself."[11]

His career as a full-time journalist had been short-lived, lasting only about a year. He would continue to practice journalism throughout his life, intermittently, to help eke out his meager income. To be true to himself, however, he felt obliged to leave his incipient career and to go on in a fresh direction, away from his home in the Rhineland. He was about to take on the life of an emigrant, an exile, as well as of a professional revolutionary.

He took two important things with him from his journalistic career: content and style. The content was a new interest in economic matters, which would underlie his shift from idealism to materialism, and become his new critical focus. The style was an increasingly polemical tone to his writings. A natural bent in Marx, already evident in the stridency of his doctoral dissertation, the polemic note was encouraged by the immediate controversial nature of his journalistic undertakings. A major result was that the esoteric, "scholarly" Marx also learned to write more direct and stinging prose, aimed at a larger "mass." Some of the fruits of his journalistic work can be savored in *The Communist Manifesto*.

Leaving Germany in 1843, Marx emigrated to Paris with high hopes. He expected to continue earning his living as a journalist, having entered into an agreement with Arnold Ruge to serve as a co-editor of a new periodical at a salary of 550 thaler a year (with Ruge putting up most of the money for the new publication). The promised income meant that Marx could now end his long courtship of Jenny, and the two were married a few months later in Kreuznach, where Jenny's mother resided (Ludwig had died in 1842), and then went off immediately for an extended honeymoon.

Once returned, Marx spent three months back at his mother-in-law's house, in Kreuznach, preparing articles for the new review. It was to be called the *Deutsch-Französische Jahrbücher* (the German-French Annals), emphasizing in its title its intended purpose of going beyond national differences. It was a first step to the internationalism that Marx embraced so fervently. As he was to tell the "workers of the world," they had no ties to any country, only to one another. This was certainly becoming Marx's own situation, as he entered on the life of an exile, a "man without a country."

As a premonition of the difficulties in achieving this aim, the *Jahrbücher* appeared without a single French contributor: the French were either suspicious of or opposed to the German metaphysicians supporting the new periodical. Indeed, the *Jahrbücher* only succeeded in appearing once, in its one-sided form, though in a double number. That single issue, however, contained three seminal articles, two by Marx and one by Engels. Marx's were "On the Jewish Question" and "Contribution to the Critique of Hegel's *Philosophy of Right:* Introduction," and Engels' on "Outlines of a Critique of Political Economy"; Marx was sufficiently impressed by the latter so as to revise his earlier unfavorable opinion of Engels, and to enter into long discussions, lasting for ten straight days, when the latter came to Paris, thus laying the basis for the most successful and significant intellectual collaboration of perhaps all times.

The French government was less impressed. Or, rather, it was impressed, but unfavorably, with the *Deutsch-Französische Jahrbücher's* main contributors, Karl Marx and Arnold Ruge. On 25 January 1845, Guizot, Minister of Interior in Louis-Philippe's bourgeois government, expelled Marx, Ruge, and others now connected with a new, twice-weekly publication, *Vorwärts*—the *Jahrbücher* had ceased publication—from France, the home of revolution. Marx was thus out of a job, as well as a place to live.

Marx and his family—for their first child, Jenny, was born in 1844, and another, Laura, was on her way—moved to Brussels. Fortunately, Marx had received an additional one thousand thalers from the *Rhein-*

ische Zeitung, as "severance pay," and this plus his savings from his *Jahrbücher* salary, and money derived from the sale of furniture, etc., meant a temporary cease to his financial problems. He would be able to devote the next three years in Brussels to study and writing. The main meaning of his expulsion from France, therefore, meant a re-confirmation that his career as a full-time journalist was not to be successful. A new career, that of professional revolutionary, stretched ahead of him. The ideas first sketched in his contributions to the *Jahrbücher* would now be increasingly connected to a theory about action, and to action itself.

IV

As a revolutionary, Marx's major activities found form in his writings; these, as in the case of other great "religious" leaders, make up the "permanent revolution" he left behind him. He was not a Robespierre or a Lenin, more important for their deeds than for their thoughts (though the latter are not to be underestimated, especially in the case of Lenin).

It is not that Marx didn't try to be a revolutionary in deed as well as word. Events were simply not propitious. The revolution which he expected to arise in Germany in the mid-forties didn't break out as planned, and when it did, in 1848, it petered out into ashes. Before that, in 1846, he and Engels had begun the German Correspondence Committee, which maintained contact among communists throughout Europe, and may be seen as the forerunner of the future communist internationals. The next year the two men organized a German Workers' Society, and also became involved in the affairs of the League of the Just, the most radical of the German secret societies, whose inspiration derived from Blanqui, but then frittered down to the non-violent communitarianism of Etienne Cabet. It was for this society that Marx and Engels would write *The Communist Manifesto* in late 1847–early 1848.

While attempting to build the German Workers' Society, Marx was also trying to arm the workers in Brussels for revolution, using some of the money from his father's legacy for this purpose. For his pains, Marx was expelled from Brussels. Moving quickly to Paris, where the revolution had originally broken out, he sought to play the same role there; subsequently, he moved on to Cologne to provide leadership in his native land. As was his wont, he established a new periodical, the *Neue Rheinische Zeitung*, as the vehicle for leading the revolution. Marx was firmly convinced that to call on the workers to rise against authority without any strictly scientific ideas or constructive doctrines was to *mislead* them. A union of theory and practice was necessary.

As the revolution began to fail and the conservative forces regained the upperhand, Marx was arrested and tried for subversion in Cologne. A brilliant speech to the jury secured his acquittal and freedom. Nevertheless, in May 1849 he was expelled from Prussia. The *Neue Rheinische Zeitung* closed down, with Marx losing about seven thousand thaler in the process. He was personally broke. Undeterred, he hastened to South Germany and then back to Paris to aid the fading revolution. By July, 1849, ordered out of France by the government, finally acknowledging the failure of the "deed," he left for London. It was to be his home for the rest of his life.

Marx hungered for an actual revolution, and involvement in it, for the remainder of his days. His mind told him that the revolution was not yet fully developed in the womb of history; his emotions cried out for its coming, and grasped at any sign of its possible birth. Thus, he anticipated its arrival in 1857 and 1863, and in 1871 he tried to see an embryonic communist revolution in the Paris Commune. Mostly, however, he settled for the task of working out the theory of the coming revolution—its scientific dimensions—and from 1864 to 1872, of founding and fighting for control of the International Working Men's Association. By then, his days at the barricades were over, memories to be drawn upon in talking to émigré conspirators or when the books in the British Museum threatened to strangulate him with their dust.

Marx, then, was an active revolutionary *manqué*. He had the character of a professional revolutionary, but not the fate. I will argue, however, that his character, as expressed in his writings, was, in part, inspirational for revolutionaries of the deed, such as Lenin, who came after. As I have theorized elsewhere, the character of a "revolutionary ascetic" is propitious for leadership in a revolution.[12] By a revolutionary ascetic, I mean one who abjures "wine, woman [the phrase is obviously sexist], and song" and any emotional ties and dedicates all his energies—"sublimates his libidinal impulses" is how I put it—to an abstraction: the People, Humanity, the Revolution. He becomes, in short, a full-time professional revolutionary, with no other attachments.

Clearly, Marx does not appear a revolutionary ascetic—at first glance. He was a loving husband and father, he had a close attachment to Engels, and he liked the good things of life.

Closer examination suggests some qualification to the objections just listed. Marx did love his family; but he was aware of the price paid, both by them and by his own revolutionary activity, because of this tie. As he remarked to his future son-in-law, Paul Lafargue, he had "sacrificed all . . . [his] . . . fortune to the revolutionary struggle" without regret, but, had he the choice to make again, he would not have married. As one commentator, David McLellan, states, "And, indeed, the price of Marx's vocation was high: of his seven children (one died at birth) only two survived him, and both of these committed suicide."[13]

In fact, within the context of his family, Marx did devote his life, single-mindedly, to revolution. Revolution was his vocation; philosophy and journalism merely adjuncts to its exercise. By his total dedication and personal sacrifice of self and loved ones, Marx impressed those around him with his apparent disinterestedness. Like the proletariat that he extolled, he appeared to have no interest different from the common interest, which it represented in principle. His father's claim of egoism, of self-interest, was thus rejected and repudiated in Marx's mind, as well as his followers', by his complete devotion to the well-being of mankind (as he saw it).

Marx's total dedication was matched by his total conviction. Part of his power over followers was the certainty he offered them as to the rightness of their mission and the doctrines guiding them. Disciples could follow him without fear of insecurity. Though he claimed his favorite maxim was "to doubt everything," Marx brooked no doubts, and could thereby silence those of his followers.

Was Marx a "totalitarian" (the word itself did not exist before the 20th century; thus, its usage in regard to Marx is, in some ways, anachronistic), whose doctrines led, and lead, inevitably to totalitarianism? A scholarly as well as polemic debate has raged over this question. I cite two respected scholars for illustrative purposes. On one side, Jacob Talmon speaks of "totalitarian democracy" and lists Marx along with Rousseau as one of its main inspirations. What Talmon has in mind is mainly a totalitarian mentality: "a state of mind, a way of feeling, a disposition . . . best compared to a set of attitudes engendered by a religion."[14]

On the other side is the work, for example, of Richard N. Hunt. I shall accord it much more attention, for it allows us to exhibit both sides of the argument fully. In his *The Political Ideas of Marx and Engels* (1974), Hunt exhaustively marshalls the evidence against the view of Marx as a totalitarian. As he correctly remarks, "chiliastic expectation—whether secular or religious—need not inevitably lead to totalitarian conclusions, else one would have to cast an entire pantheon of Jewish prophets and Christian saints in the hellfire of political perdition."[15] More positively, Hunt argues that what Marx "envisaged for the future society, from its very beginning, was a kind of participatory democracy organized without any professional leaders or administrators at all, which has nowhere been established in a national government. . . ."

Marx, Hunt argues, took for granted the existence of political rights, i.e., the "rights of man" of the French Revolution. (In fact, this is not quite accurate; Marx drew a distinction between the rights of man, which are "egoistic," and the rights of the citizen.) Marx wished, however, to go beyond them, as we will see in "On the Jewish Question," to human emancipation. In fact, the French Revolution itself had gone beyond the rights of man, though not towards humanism, in its aftermath, in The Conspiracy of Equals of 1796–97. Babeuf and his followers advocated, Hunt reminds us, "the need for a vanguard party, a minority revolution, an educational dictatorship by an elite possessing a monopoly of the means of coercion and communication, wholesale terror, and mass politicization." As Hunt concedes, "Such a program can be called totalitarian without robbing the word of its distinctive twentieth-century meaning"; it is the program Talmon recognized as " 'crystallized totalitarian' democracy."[16]

Babeuf's views were taken up by Blanqui, and it is this Babouvist-Blanquist prescription for minority revolution and totalitarian dictatorship, Hunt claims, that has been attributed to Marx. Though, Hunt admits, Marx was tempted in the 1848–50 period by this view, he did not finally subscribe to it. Quite the contrary. Similarly, almost a century and a half after the French Revolution and its Babouvism is 20th-century Marxism, and Hunt concludes that this, too, is a distortion of Marx's position: "Insofar as Marxism has become, in the twentieth century, a doctrine exploited by the alienated intelligentsia of underdeveloped countries to win support for, and justify, their own modernizing dictatorships, the idea of the vanguard and of educational rule necessarily came to play a role which had no foundation in original Marxism and which harked back to the earlier tradition of Babeuf and Blanqui.

Marx and Engels must thus be distinguished not only from this earlier tradition but from most of their twentieth-century 'followers,' as holding to the ultimate democratic conviction that the emancipation of the masses intrinsically must be the work of the masses themselves."[17]

In sum, Hunt defends Marx from the allegations of totalitarianism, explaining why they have been made, and ends up depicting Marx as a participatory democrat. We need, very briefly, both to reexamine and evaluate the evidence. Marx, following upon his father and his second-father, Ludwig von Westphalen, was at first a liberal democrat and even a monarchist. He quickly moved beyond this position, as he encountered the reality of the reactionary and intransigent Prussian state. It is that state that colored his views on political possibilities and influenced his eventual decision to advocate the abolition of the state. Before going on, we must call attention to Marx's own premonitions of the disastrous consequences of such an aspiration. In 1842, while still a liberal democrat, he wrote an article (never published during his life) discussing the view of his friend, the socialist Moses Hess, that the state would one day disappear: "Philosophy must seriously protest when it is confused with imagination," Marx declared. As if echoing the words of his school essay on choosing a vocation, warning of the lures of abstract thought, he cautioned that such ideas constitute a "real danger" if they capture the hearts of men. Communist aspirations amount to a "rebellion of man's subjective wishes against his objective understanding."[18]

With the Prussian reality before him, however, Marx began to move in a "subjective" direction. While acknowledging that American republicanism was preferable to Prussian authoritarianism, he also wrote that "the entire content of law and the state is, with small modification, the same in North America as in Prussia . . . The content of the state lies outside these constitutions."[19] Similarly, he rejected Hegel's view of the bureaucracy as an unselfish "universal class." Against both American republicanism and Prussian bureaucratically administered statism, Marx turned back to the ideal of the Greek polis. Here he saw the *res publica* as the immediate concern of each citizen, whose participation made it possible to conduct public business without a bureaucracy or any other body standing outside civil society. The flaw, of course, was slavery; but Marx saw industrial society as making slavery—wage as well as legal—unnecessary. Communist society, therefore, could be "stateless," without any professional administrators (division of labor, after all, will be abolished), or political parties.

On this view, Marx is clearly not totalitarian-minded. It must be said immediately, however, that some scholars do not agree with Hunt's dismissal of Marx's "Blanquist" qualities, or his relegation of them to a single period, 1844–50, and then their complete disappearance. I myself am arguing that Marx's revolutionary aspirations, his desire for revolution *now*, stood as a recurrent temptation. The case for and against Marx's Blanquism is, nevertheless, inconclusive; as such, it cannot be grounds for concluding that Marx is a totalitarian.

The question remains whether there was something in either Marx's character or doctrines that had a tendency to inspire others to a totalitarian outcome. Is it that, although not himself a totalitarian thinker, the eschatological aspirations in Marx led him to a lack of realism concerning man and society which made for a lacuna into which totalitarian solutions rushed? Did Marx himself sense this possibility in his remarks of 1842 on Moses Hess? On Marx's own terms, industrial society is very different from the Greek polis, vastly more complex and stratified. If simple Greek society was, in fact, characterized by political parties and upheavals leading to the Aristotelian cycle of despotism, monarchy, aristocracy, democracy, and back to despotism, why assume that our more complicated society would be different?

As we shall see in more detail, Marx's response was that social stratification would be done away with when the increasing polarization into capitalists and proletariats resulted in the collapse (or uprising) of all strata into one, classless society. By Marx's definition, state and political parties are the products of private property; its abolition does away with them as well. To a non-Marxist (and perhaps to a Marxist as well), all this is a matter of faith—and of eschatological faith. The problem with saying that there will be no more political parties, however, is that anyone who wishes to present it that way can say that a single party, defined as representing all the people, i.e., the proletariat, is the same as no party. This, in fact, is the sleight of logic pulled by all totalitarian parties.

Another problem is that Marx assumed that history—the "laws" of economic development—would lead the proletariat to educate, organize, and liberate itself. What if things didn't work out that way? Marx the philosopher might advocate patience. Marx the revolutionary might have difficulty in waiting, especially since in the advanced industrialist countries, capitalist reform, however grudgingly given, was heading off proletarian revolution; and if Marx didn't have this difficulty, followers like Lenin did. Consequently, communists became a vanguard party, taking over the state by Blanquist means, and then claiming to educate the proletariat to eventually assume rulerless rule. In the interval, the dictatorship of the proletariat was not in the hands of the proletariat.

Even if Marx did not positively have a "totalitarian mentality," as Talmon alleges, his naïveté about human nature, society, and politics (oddly combined as it is with great realism and acumen) led him to be one of the "terribles simplificateurs" of history, to use the phrase of the Swiss historian Jacob Burckhardt. Must such simplification lead to totalitarianism? Might it when linked to a millennial impatience? The view that history is a struggle between good and evil, with no humanity attributed to those assigned to the latter camp, moves us, according to Erik Erikson, in the direction of what he calls Allness or Nothingness, which he finds conducive to totalitarianism.

I myself am convinced that Marx thought of himself as a democrat. Yet, while in his early writings he partly accepted the concept of the rights of man as a dialectical advance while criticizing its limitations; he gave no regard anywhere in his work to the protection of individual rights—for he assumed that in communist society there would be no need for such protection. He does not move in the tradition of a John Locke, a James Madison, or a John Stuart Mill, with their concern for a system of checks and balances on the human proclivity to power; their definition of "liberty" and Marx's is far apart. Consequently, there are no safeguards in Marx's doctrines against the possible rise of totalitarianism. A Lenin, therefore, could speak easily in the name of Marx. If those who advocate what is called "Socialism with a Human Face" seek to oppose Stalinism, they must find an alternate political philosophy, and institutions, in a source other than Marx, who offers none.

Marx wished a communist revolution. Its result was not to be a totalitarian society, but one in which the "free development of each is the condition for the free development of all." This was Marx's definition of humanism; it quickly turned into "scientific socialism" in his work. In turn, the latter predicts an inevitable reality which is, in fact, utopian. And utopia, a "nowhere," could be transformed, under certain circumstances not freely chosen by men, into the "everywhere" of totalitarianism.

V

What about Marx the man, as well as philosopher? Was there that in his character, as well as in his doctrines, which might accord with a drift to totalitarianism? I have described him as having the character of a professional revolutionary. As such, did he also have a "dictatorial" character? We have much testimony to this effect. A few examples must suffice. The Russian liberal, Pavel Annenkov, observed in 1846, on meeting Marx, "He always spoke in imperative words that would brook no contradiction and were made all the sharper by the almost painful impression of the tone which ran through everything he said. This tone expressed the firm conviction of his mission to dominate men's minds and prescribe them their laws. Before me stood the embodiment of a democratic dictator such as one might imagine in a day dream." Carl Schurz, the German émigré to America after the failure of the 1848 revolution, described the thirty-year-old Marx as follows: "To no opinion which differed from his own did he accord the honour of even condescending consideration. Everyone who contradicted him he treated with abject contempt; every argument that he did not like he answered either with biting scorn at the unfathomable ignorance that had prompted it, or with opprobrious aspersions upon the motives of him who had advanced it."[20]

We could cite many more such descriptions and statements. They are of a piece with similar descriptions of future followers of Marx, such as Lenin. Thus a thirty-year-old Russian Marxist commented on Lenin:

"No one could so fire others with their plans, no one could so impose his will and conquer by force of his personality . . . only Lenin represented that rare phenomenon, especially rare in Russia, of a man of iron will and indomitable energy who combines fanatical faith in the movement, the cause, with no less faith in himself . . . [he] had the feeling that in him the will of the movement was concentrated in one man. And he acted accordingly."[21]

The same terms seem to apply to Marx, leading us to wonder whether indeed his personality and ideas may have served as a prototype or inspiration.

Needless to say, there are many differences between Marx and Lenin as personalities. Marx was, for example, fun-loving, absent-minded, and slovenly in a way foreign to Lenin. But the similarities give us some hint as to what kind of "revolutionary ascetic" in "deed" Marx might have been if fate and history had so conspired. Instead, Marx became a teacher of revolutionaries rather than a successful revolutionary himself. He was a dictatorial teacher. We have many accounts of how his determined personality—what his opponents might call his dogmatism—overwhelmed his pupils. He lectured at them, gave them "examinations," and treated them, even when his own age, as, in the words of Wilhelm Liebknecht, "young fellows."

Yet, with all this said, we cannot leap from "dictatorial" elements in Marx's character to portraying him as a totalitarian. We cannot be sure that the demands of a revolutionary situation such as he advocated—his was not the revolution of a George Washington or a Thomas Jefferson—would or would not have moved Marx in the direction of authoritarianism, and then totalitarianism. The other elements in his character and doctrines—his anti-authoritarian and Promethean-like humanistic qualities, for example—might have halted such a slide. There was nothing in Marx's overall character, however, combined with the "simplifications" of his doctrines, which would prevent some of his disciples from feeling that they were "in character," i.e., in *his* character, in making the "dictatorship of the proletariat" a totalitarian dictatorship.

Marx, if the Prussian government would have allowed him, would have been a Professor of Philosophy. Instead, he became a Professor of Revolution. Nevertheless, his character was in many ways that of an active revolutionary, a Promethean of the streets, setting fire to the altars of authority. As it turned out, his fight against authority was to be carried out mainly by words, in his writings. By accepting his vocation as a revolutionary in thought, Marx, paradoxically, also became the most successful revolutionary in practice of all time.

It is to the writings, then, that one must turn to understand Marx the man who chose to become a revolutionary, even if not under circumstances chosen by himself. As he remarked in "The Eighteenth Brumaire of Louis Bonaparte," "Men make their own history, but they do not make it just as they believe . . . but under circumstances directly found, given and transmitted from the past. The tradition of all the dead generations weigh like a nightmare on the brain of the living."[22] Out of his personal nightmare Marx made an historical revolution in the future circumstances of millions of human beings.

VI

Marx With a Human Face

In the autumn of 1843, when he was 25 years old and living with his new bride, Jenny, Marx wrote "On the Jewish Question," basing the work on two articles on the subject of Bruno Bauer, and, as was Marx's wont, quoting liberally in order to establish the grounds of his own critique.* Marx is already implicitly critical of his erstwhile mentor, Bauer, and will finish off the job a few years later in *The Holy Family* (written with Engels), which is a turgid diatribe against Bauer and his two brothers; however, in "On the Jewish Question," the tone is still respectful. This essay, published in the *Deutsch-Französische Jahrbücher*, is important as a stage in Marx's development of his overall theory, but it is also significant as showing how Marx tried to liberate himself from the "Jewish Question" and how he tried to liberate the Jews from their religion.

---

*Critique was a favored German word. Whereas English thinkers wrote "Inquiries" (or "Enquiries")—one thinks of Locke, Hume, Adam Smith—philosophers in Germany, such as Kant and Hegel, wrote "Critiques" (e.g., Kant's *Critique of Pure Reason*). By critique they meant a reexamination of fundamental assumptions previously taken as givens, rather than an inquiry on empirical lines, in an effort to establish principles and theories. Marx was in the line of critiques, e.g., not taking for granted the nature of religion, or private property, but critically examining their validity as initial assumptions. As he moved into the field of economics, he sought to combine the "inquiry" approach, as in *Capital*, with critique.

Bauer's argument was that Jews were unrealistic and inconsistent in wanting political emancipation *as Jews*, i.e., while retaining their religion. Either they must seek support from liberal Germans, i.e., men like Bruno Bauer, who have themselves abandoned religion, albeit the Christian belief, and who expect the same action from the Jews for whom they are fighting; or they must appeal to the believing Christians for support, whose very belief entails an adherence to the view that only the Christian religion is the correct one for the state and will therefore oppose Jews as such from having the rights of citizens.

The solution, according to Bauer, is that the Jews renounce Judaism and that all men renounce religion in order to be citizens. The political abolition of religion, i.e., a privileged religion, means, for him, the abolition of all religion.

This is Bauer's main argument. Marx, in good Hegelian fashion, wants to transcend it critically. He starts by accepting his friend's wish to abolish religion in general. To end religious opposition between Christian and Jew, one abolishes religion. As Marx puts it, "As soon as Jew and Christian come to see in their respective religions nothing more than *stages in the development of the human mind . . .* they will no longer find themselves in religious opposition, but in a purely critical, *scientific* and human relationship."[1] Adding an emphasis to Bauer's idea, Marx continues, "Science will then constitute their unity. But scientific oppositions are resolved by science itself." Such a statement is very Hegelian, with a touch of Saint-Simonian positivism hanging over it, and it is evocative of Marx's own stages of development from Jew to Christian to "scientist." Marx's "Science," in short, can end the strife of Jew and Christian in the real, as well as personal, world. It is, for him, a liberating force.

Marx then goes well beyond Bauer. First, Marx states, it is not true, as Bauer asserts, that true political emancipation means the end of religion: the United States is proof that a politically free country can also have a flourishing system of private religions. Bauer's limitation is that he stops at political and religious emancipation, but does not examine the relation between political and *human* emancipation. In order to understand what is involved in the latter freedom, one must understand the relations of state and civil society. The motivating force of civil society, or what we would call the economic sphere, is the "egoistic life," i.e., materialism. The relation of civil society to the state bears close examination, Marx asserts, for the state sees man as living in a community and civil society sees man as being a private individual, whose interests may be opposed to the general interest. In the "Jewish" essay, Marx is rather cloudy on this subject, but he will write later with scathing clarity as to how the state is merely the political embodiment of society's ruling class. Here he has only vague intimations.

He sees the perfected political state as representing man as a species-being, i.e., above egoism, and in opposition to egoism. A contradiction, therefore, exists. In very murky fashion, Marx describes what will later become a central part of his scientific theory of social development: material changes bring about political and intellectual changes, although the political turns at times on the civil in cannibalistic fashion, as during the Reign of Terror. "At those times," he writes, "when the state is most aware of itself, political life seeks to stifle its own prerequisites—civil society and its elements—and to establish itself as the genuine and harmonious species-life of man. But it can only achieve this end by setting itself in violent contradiction with its own conditions of existence, by declaring a *permanent revolution*."

Political life is merely a reflected, or alienated, state of man. His real life is in tangible, material existence. Thus, Marx declares, "We do not say to the Jews, therefore, as does Bauer: you cannot be emancipated politically, without emancipating yourselves completely from Judaism. We say rather: it is because you can be emancipated politically, without renouncing Judaism completely and absolutely, that *political emancipation* itself is not *human* emancipation. If you want to be politically emancipated, without emancipating yourselves humanly, the inadequacy and the contradiction is not entirely in yourselves but in the *nature* and the *category* of political emancipation."

Now political emancipation by itself was, Marx conceded, a form of "great progress." What he saw, however, was that this progress was the *result* of changes in civil society, not a cause in itself. The problem with political revolution per se is that "it dissolves civil society into its elements without *revolutionizing* these elements themselves or subjecting them to criticism." Bauer had stopped at religious and political criticism and revolution—and had not seen that they are merely the tail on the dog.

How are we to go beyond Bauer? At this point we must go back to the beginning of Marx's article and recognize that there is an undercurrent to Bauer's writing that colors the logic with a heavy emotional tone. In fact, Marx's first quote, at the very beginning of his own article, touches on this part of Bauer's message. "You Jews," Bauer writes, "are *egoists* if you demand for yourselves as Jews, a special emancipation. You should work, as Germans for the political emancipation of Germany, and as men, for the emancipation of mankind." Such a statement seems an uncanny echo of some of Marx's father's letters, without the attribution of "Jews" to the charge. I have tried to show how Marx dealt with his father's accusation. With Bauer the matter takes on another form, although, I am arguing, a connected form. Heinrich Marx had converted to Christianity; Bauer would have urged him to go further. As Bauer wrote, "If they wish to become free the Jews should not embrace Christianity as such, but Christianity in dissolution, religion in dissolution; that is to say, the Enlightenment, criticism, and its outcome, a free humanity." In short, Jews should convert to atheism.

Marx, pursuing the theme of human, and not just religious, emancipation, takes another tack. "What specific *social* element," he asks, "is it necessary to overcome in order to abolish Judaism?" To find the answer, he continues, "Let us consider the real Jew: not the *sabbath Jew* whom Bauer considers, but the *everyday Jew*." Marx's conclusion is devastating: "What is the profane basis of Judaism? *Practical* need, *self-interest*. What is the worldly cult of the Jew? *Huckstering*. What is his worldly god? *Money*."

What is so striking is that Marx has reified individual Jews, some of whom may be engaged in monied activities, into *The Jew*, and thus accepted all of the stereotypes placed on this entity by anti-Semites. When he adds that in Judaism we find "a universal *antisocial* element" whose eradication—Marx's word is "emancipation"—will emancipate all mankind, we are close to the ravings of an Adolf Hitler.

I am *not* saying—repeat, not—that Marx was a Nazi, or even an anti-Semite as such. (In fact, shortly before his article, Marx had supported a petition to the Rhenish Diet, the purpose of which was to do away with the remaining legal discriminations against Jews.)[2] He would probably have recoiled violently from the "practice" of his thought; however, his thought does lend itself to misuse by later doers of deeds. What Marx was saying, overtly, was that Judaism is a synonym for capitalism. At its core is money: "Money is the jealous god of Israel, beside which no other god may exist. Money abases all the gods of mankind and changes them into commodities. Money is the alienated essence of man's work and existence; this essence dominates him and he worships it." These are the same terms Marx uses to describe capitalism in his *Economic and Philosophic Manuscripts*.

Marx, who overtly abjured nationalism, and had no ostensible nationality of his own, wrote: "The *chimerical* nationality of the Jew is the nationality of the trader, and above all of the financier." Thus, he echoes the charge that Jew and capitalist are without loyalty to the nation, unrooted in the land, and quick to take their liquid gold—money—anywhere they can make a profit.

Christianity would *appear* to overcome and do away with this essence of Judaism. But Marx prefers to read history as a matter of Judaism attaining "universal domination" through the very universality of Christianity, with the latter being merely "the sublime thought of Judaism," which retains its "vulgar, practical" nature. God and money are identical, as are Christianity and Judaism, in that both are sources of alienation: we create these artificial beings and then allow them to dominate us; thus we are alienated from ourselves. To abolish our alienated existence, we must do away with the existence of Judaism (and, by an implication, not intended by Marx, actual Jews?) as well as of religion. "The social emancipation of the Jew," Marx concludes, "is the *emancipation of society from Judaism*."

The essay "On the Jewish Question" is an extraordinary work. It combines the embryos of many of Marx's most important and penetrating mature theories with a farrago of nonsense and almost incredibly bad reasoning. Many commentators have been content to emphasize the incipient theories, and dismiss the rest as a lapse of sorts. Others have read it as lamentable anti-Semitic utterances, and nothing more important. I suggest that a closer, more connected, reading of the two parts is essential.

By now, words such as "egoism" and "money" in Marx's writings must always alert us to their personal meanings for him. A commonplace in the culture of his time, the words and the arguments about them, I am arguing, have additional and special meaning for him. So does the "Jewish Question," and anything to do with Christianity and religion in general. Marx may, and does, hide this from himself; there is no reason for it to be hidden from us.

We noticed earlier Marx's use of the phrase "self-contempt" in his essay on choosing a vocation. Why and how would a seventeen-year-old boy know about such feelings? we asked. His father had accused him of being egoistic and possibly demon-driven against mankind. Money was a source of discord between the two men. As a Jew, though a Christian, Marx was open to the criticism of anti-Semites that Jews were self-interested hucksters, whose interests were adverse both to the nation and to humanity. These are all matters of potential self-loathing. To restore a sense of an esteemed self, how better than to identify with the criticisms, project them outward, and in a critical spirit, reject them and call for their abolition?**

In so doing, if I am right, Karl Marx also stumbled on toward his fruitful insights about society, capitalism, and history. He, who was alienated from his self, could glimpse the nature of alienation in society. He could understand that religion, and the state, were to be perceived in relation to the society from which they sprang and on which they stood. He could realize that changes in civil society, whose latest form was the capitalist, meant changes in the rest of the social structure and culture. Alienation, religion, capitalism, these were the staples of intellectual discourse at the time; Marx's genius was to give them a new, and personal, twist.***

In a piece of exceptionally poor history, Marx equated the Jew with the coming of capitalism. (In fact, the Jew was on the margin of this development; Marx himself dropped the identification later on in his work, and spent the rest of his life trying to abolish both.) The paradox is that, in the process, he became an outstanding historian of capitalism and of the industrial society it helped to create.

** Marx himself was attacked by some of his opponents as a Jew, in spite of his upbringing as a Christian. In turn, he used less than judicious epithets in regard to some of his opponents, often former allies, who happened to be Jewish. Thus, in letters to Engels, he mocked his "friend", Lassalle, and called him "the Jewish Nigger." Engels also made insulting racial comments about Jews, showing an insensitivity to his friend's family background; Marx's only response was to "up" his friend's epithets. Both Marx and Engels also showed an obdurate prejudice toward the Slavs, making disparaging racial remarks about them as well.[3] An explanation such as the one I am offering can make sense out of Marx's anti-Semitic language, which, while typical of many non-Jews of the time—part of the "climate of opinion"—requires special explanation for one of Marx's background.

*** By showing the personal roots of Marx's ideas—the correspondence of his life and thought—I am not invalidating the philosophical source of these ideas, which operate on him simultaneously with his lived experience. To explain, is not to explain away. My project is not to reduce Marx and his writings to one strand, but to enrich our understanding of a multi-stranded development—and consequent meaning.

II

In the writings that follow the "Jewish Question," the personal note grows less and less obvious. It is there, but Marx has settled a major score and can now distance himself, intellectually, from it. The introduction to the "Contribution to the Critique of Hegel's *Philosophy of Right*," written in that burst of creative energy in the fall of 1843, right after his marriage, serves as a bridge to Marx's increasingly intellectualized work.

The centrality of the religious question, if not the Jewish one, is still the starting point. "The criticism of religion," Marx announces in the first sentence, "is the premise of all criticism."[4] Besides Hegel, Marx had now also been reading Ludwig Feuerbach—indeed, he sent a copy of his essay to him, accompanying it with a long letter of admiration—and it is Feuerbach's influence that can be felt in the next assertion that "*man makes religion*; religion does not make man." It is only a short step to the future claim that "men make their history. . . ."

More specifically, Marx continues, "state . . . [and] society, produce religion which is an *inverted world consciousness*, because they are an *inverted world*." What Marx has in mind is the Feuerbachian idea that man, rather than being created in the image of God, creates God in his own image, i.e., out of real, earthly needs and desires. Religion is a matter of anthropology, not theology, for Feuerbach.

We ought also to note the centrality of perspective for Marx. Here, and constantly elsewhere, he is claiming that the world is seen upside down. He draws his inspiration from Feuerbach's idea of "transformational criticism," which consists in the inversion of a philosophy's principal propositions, i.e., the transposition of subject and predicate. The connection to a chiastic style, which we noted before, is plain. Marx made the "inverted" attitude peculiarly his own. Even Hegel must be stood right side up. Marx is out to make an optical revolution. His historical telescope is based on inversion of the image. He wants us to see that we have mistaken for reality what is only illusion, and an illusion created by ourselves at that. Plato had spoken of shadows in the cave made by a fire whose flickers we mistake for the true fire of the sun. Marx will have us look directly at the sun.

Religion as the illusory happiness of men must be abolished. Marx's famous statement that religion "is the *opium* of the people" follows on his assertion that religion is both an expression of real suffering and a protest against it.# Freed from illusions, men, no longer duped, will no longer need to be doped. The task of history will be to establish "the *truth of this world.*" The task of philosophy, which serves history, is to unmask that type of human self-alienation which has taken the form of religion, by critique, and to do the same, by the same means, with the secular form, i.e., of state and society; religious criticism leads to political (and economic) criticism.

We hear no more of religion in this essay. Marx moves on to philosophy and politics. He concerns himself with Germany, and with the hoped for revolution in that country. A strong touch of nationalist feeling shows itself, even though Marx is on the point of becoming a man without a country.

With some disgust, he remarks that Germany in 1843 is politically still at the level of France in pre-revolutionary 1789; Germany's only pride is that, philosophically, it is the most advanced nation. Industrially, it is just starting out. Marx does not compare it to England, the leading economic country, in this essay; the fact that he ignores the foremost industrial example is a measure of his German parochialism in 1843, as well as of his lack of knowledge of economic theory and data. Marx, himself, in 1843, is at the level of Germany.

Marx puts all this in dramatic terms. The French *ancien régime*, he says, played a tragic part in history; i.e., it led to a real revolution. In Germany, it plays a comic part, i.e., 1843 Germany is at the level of the actual *ancien régime*, but will produce no bourgeois revolution. "The modern *ancien régime*," Marx announces, "is the comedian of a world order whose *real heroes* are dead." Marx then raises this particular statement to a general one about world history, "The last stage of a world-historical formation is comedy. The Greek gods, already once mortally wounded in Aeschylus' tragedy *Prometheus Bound*, had to endure a second death, a comic death, in Lucian's dialogues. Why should history proceed in this way? So that mankind shall separate itself gladly from its past." He ends by applying this "law" again to his immediate subject. "We claim this *joyful* historical destiny for the political powers of Germany."

Let us pause over this use by Marx of images from drama. He will use them, and specifically this one, throughout his work. The most fa-

#As a matter of historical fact, religion at the time can also be said to have been the opium of the bourgeoisie; see, for example, Elizabeth Gaskell's *Mary Barton*, and her religious message, discussed in Chapter I.

mous instance is probably the opening lines of "The Eighteenth Brumaire," where he writes that "Hegel remarks somewhere that all great, world-historical facts and personages occur, as it were, twice. He has forgotten to add: the first time as tragedy, the second as farce." ## Marx, the aspiring dramatist, the writer of the half-finished *Oulanem*, is now the playwright for a wider stage, world history.

The second act of the drama—the first is the religious—is philosophical. Germany, we are told, though backward practically, is ahead in thought. How can it "connect its dream historically with its present conditions"? Marx asks. The first part of the answer is at hand: philosophy, like religion, must be dealt with critically. With this accomplished, and Marx is at the forefront of the task, critical philosophy must itself then be abolished. The task of theory is to lead to a practical realization, which absorbs philosophy in actuality.

The specific problem Marx is wrestling with is whether Germany, backward as it is practically, can skip a stage—a political revolution à la 1789—and jump to a more advanced revolution: "The question then arises: can Germany attain a practical activity à la hauteur des principes; that is to say, a revolution which will raise it not only to the official level of the modern nations, but to the human level which will be the immediate future of those nations."

Marx thrashes to and fro over his answer. The philosophy of history, whose outlines he was beginning to perceive, seemed to call for a dialectical development which required a bourgeois revolution, as had occurred in France, or at least supremacy, which would then prepare the conditions for a further revolution. As Marx puts it, "A radical revolution can only be a revolution of radical needs, for which the conditions and breeding ground appear to be lacking."

The young Marx was too eager, however, for a revolution *now* to be content with such a prosaic answer. His own experience in 1842 had shown him how weak, and even servile, the bourgeoisie was in Germany; one could not expect a revolution from their likes. They were simply not up to playing their historical role. A new actor—or hero—must be found, and the bourgeoisie given a new, actually secondary, role.

The new actor was the proletariat. Although its lines were already

In fact, Marx is misquoting or has misread Hegel, who says more or less the opposite. See my piece "The Tragic Farce of Marx, Hegel, and Engels: A Note", *History and Theory*, Vol. XI, No. 3, 1972.

written, Marx realized that the actor would have to be created and trained, for he did not yet exist substantially. "A class must be formed," Marx declared, "which has *radical chains*, a class in civil society which is not a class of civil society. . . ."

Marx was aware that the proletariat was "only beginning to form itself in Germany." Only if the bourgeoisie would play its assigned supporting role, be a proper villain, would the new heroic class develop. "For one class to be the liberating class *per excellence*, it is necessary that another class should be openly the oppressing class." The bourgeoisie's new role, therefore, was not itself to be an oppressed class, rising up in revolution against the feudal aristocracy, but simply an oppressing class.[5]

The sole class remaining in the ranks of the oppressed, the proletariat, would by definition embody the general interest, and have no interests of its own. In Marx's more lyrical phrasing, "There must be formed a sphere of society which claims no *traditional* status but only a human status, a sphere which is not opposed to particular consequences but is totally opposed to the assumptions of the German political system; a sphere, finally, which cannot emancipate itself without emancipating itself from all the other spheres of society, without, therefore, emancipating all these other spheres, which is, in short, a *total loss* of humanity and which can only redeem itself by a *total redemption of humanity*. This dissolution of society, as a particular class, is the *proletariat*." A cynic might sigh that Marx is more mystifying then demystifying in such passages.

Marx's totalism, so he claimed, was not a mere dream. Defending himself vigorously, and in anticipation, against such a charge, he announced, "It is not radical revolution, universal human emancipation, which is a Utopian dream for Germany, but rather a partial, merely political revolution which leaves the pillars of the building standing." Marx would pull down the entire building in real life, and not just in his dream; he would, to use the words of his early poem, "destroy a world."

The destruction would make room for "the new world which is coming into being." In this world, philosophy and action, i.e., the proletariat, would fuse. In a passage pregnant with vague longing and meaning, Marx declares, "Just as philosophy finds its material weapons in the proletariat, so the proletariat finds its intellectual weapons in philosophy. And once the lightning of thought has penetrated deeply into this virgin soil of the people, the Germans will emancipate themselves and become men. . . ." As he concludes, "Philosophy can only be realized by the abolition of the proletariat, and the proletariat can only be abolished by the realization of philosophy."

What would be the shape of this new world? Marx, on the edge of his own manhood (he was now twenty-five years old), offers little more description here other than that man will recover his humanity, or, rather, for the first time "become men." His own transient vocation, philosophy, was to be abolished, or rather fused with the real world, in the form of the proletariat.### Prometheus, carrying the "lightning of thought," was setting foot on the earth as a true revolutionary. Marx had glimpsed the novel shape revolution, his total revolution, would take; now he needed to work out the dramatic plot by which it would actually be realized in the world of men and history, rather than of dreams. The irony is that, in fact, Marx remained a revolutionary philosopher more than a philosophical revolutionary for the rest of his life.

III

In 1844, in Paris, Marx finally sought to come to grips with English economic theory, and thus to lay a material basis for his critique of Hegel. His approach to economics, though he claimed it was empirical, was still philosophical. It was Engels who described the actual workings of the factory system in Manchester in 1844 in the *Condition of the Working Class in England* (published 1845). Where Engels described slums and cesspools, Marx quoted and analyzed Adam Smith.

A few years later, for example, in "Wage Labour and Capital" of 1849, and certainly by the time of *Capital*, in 1867, Marx had fused theory and empirical observation into a single account, even if his empiricism was only in terms of Parliamentary Blue Books of inquiry into the actual

###There seems to be a pattern discernible in Marx's repudiations. Having himself given up religious belief, he calls for the destruction of all religion. Unable himself to be an academic philosopher, he demands the abolition of philosophy. It is as if he were saying, "If I can't be a philosopher, nobody will be one." The same pattern shows itself, in slightly different form, in his personal relations as well: once he has absorbed and gone past his mentors—Hegel, Bauer, Feuerbach, etc.—he must turn and destroy them. Part of Marx's enormous creativity, a lived dialectic, this pattern also seems to reflect a kind of cannibalistic trait. From yet another point of view, his behavior may be seen as founded in a fear that if he does not burn his bridges, so to speak, he may slip back or regress in some fashion.

working conditions. (The Blue Books resulted from the desire of reform-minded Members of Parliament to pass legislation dealing with factory conditions, child labor, hours of work, etc.; the data was often horrifying.) In 1844, however, Marx was still pursuing his purely critical vocation, inspired as much by Ludwig Feuerbach as by Adam Smith. The resultant manuscript remained unpublished until 1932, and appears only in the fragmentary and disorganized form in which Marx left it.

Of all his early works, the so-called *Economic and Philosophic Manuscripts of 1844*, or the "Paris" Manuscripts, has particularly served as the basis for assertions about "Socialism with a Human Face" (in my language, "Marx with a Human Face"). Here, we are told, is the "humanistic" Marx, the Marx who stressed the primacy of human existence and satisfaction rather than "laws" of historical development, whose "scientific" determinism could be distorted so as to justify a "dictatorship of the proletariat," such as can be found in the Soviet Union. Thus, East European Marxists appeal to the Marx of the 1844 manuscripts to justify their rebellion against what they view as the sterile Marxist-Leninism of Stalinist Russia.

In place of what they see as vulgar Marxism, some of these modern Marxist thinkers have emphasized the elements of humanism and alienation, in Marx's work, and have argued that alienation could exist even in a supposed Communist state such as the Soviet Union. They claim that the "young" Marx is the authentic figure who is betrayed by the "old" Marx.[6] The potential political and ideological import of this intellectual debate is clearly major. One can sympathize with the political desires without necessarily being convinced of the ideological interpretation.

I am taking the position, indeed, that there is one Marx. There is a consistency to his life and writings. Of course, he was once young, and he became old; his ideas changed and developed, and shifted in emphasis. He, and they, were always characterized by ambiguities and ambivalences: he was human. It is exactly the "human" quality of Marx that ties his work together. It is his "self," unified in its contradictions, that animates all his work, and gives it a persistent and recognizable Marxist character. "Marx with a Human face" refers, as I use the phrase, not only to a political position, relying on an emphasis on the youthful writings, but to a human being expressing his deepest feelings, wishes, and thoughts in his life work. It is in this spirit that I suggest we read the *Economic and Philosophic Manuscripts*, as well as all his other utterances.

His preface reminds us that this work is to form part of his general critique, of which the essay on Hegel's Philosophy of Right had centered on jurisprudence and political science. Promising others on laws, ethics, politics, etc., Marx adds that at the end he will present them as a connected whole (a promise never realized); meanwhile the present work is to be a critique of political economy. Marx is at some pains to guard himself against the charge of being merely speculative and utopian. "It is hardly necessary," he writes, "to assure the reader conversant with political economy that my results have been won by means of a wholly empirical analysis based on a conscientious critical study of political economy."[7]

By "empirical" he really means "positive"; and positive criticism, he declares, begins with the discoveries of Feuerbach, whose writings he rates as the only ones "since Hegel's *Phänomenologie* and *Logik* to contain a real theoretical revolution." The term "positive" is an especially troubling one as used by Marx. He is not referring to the ideas of Auguste Comte, for whom it means "scientific," i.e., going beyond the metaphysical to natural laws, and whose philosophy Marx detested.[8] Instead, he is following Feuerbach's usage.

Without going into details about Feuerbach, we can discern the meaning of "empirical." We can also note that there are overlaps between Feuerbach and Comte. Where Feuerbach announces, "my philosophy is no philosophy," the French author of *Cours de philosophie positive* could well agree with him: science replaces philosophy. But Feuerbach has something else in mind than the methods of the Scientific Revolution. *His* method "aims to achieve a continuous unification of the noble with the apparently common, of the distant with the *near-at-hand*, of the *abstract* with the *concrete*, of the *speculative* with the *empirical*, of *philosophy* with *life*. . . "[9] "Empirical" refers to sensory experience, the basis of speculation; but Feuerbach's empiricism is not the gathering of scientific facts and their use in verifying theories, but a rooting of critique in the essence of man, conceived as a creature who "is what he eats" and who creates gods in his own image. He is "materialist" man, set in opposition to Hegel's "idealist" man; and it is Feuerbach whom Marx acknowledges as guiding him as he settles accounts with Hegelian philosophy. "Positive" man, then, is the very human being being described by Marx in the *Economic and Philosophic Manuscripts*, as we shall see.

The first part of Marx's surviving manuscript quotes Adam Smith at length; it is a running commentary on *The Wealth of Nations*. It seems quite removed from either Hegel or Feuerbach, but it is a mistake not to recognize that, in discussing "Wages of Labour," "Profits of Capital," and "Rent of Land," the three component parts of Smith's theory of value, Marx has in mind other ends than the progenitor of classical economics.

The key section is on wages of labor. Marx is out to show that the increased wealth of society—of nations—means the increased poverty and degradation of the individual. The idea is certainly latent in Smith, though in the end he draws opposite conclusions. Marx, however, will have none of this faith in the ultimately benevolent outcome of the pursuit of self-interest, guided by the invisible hand of Providence—in fact, the market place—to be found in Smith. Instead, he quotes Smith only to negative purposes, and in a negative tone.

Smith had said that "In that original state of things, which precedes both the appropriation of land and the accumulation of stock, the whole produce of labor belongs to the laborer. He has neither landlord nor master to share with him." Smith then concluded that it was "to no purpose" to inquire what would be the case if the laborer kept all the gains occasioned by increased productivity resulting from the division of labor. Marx obviously thought otherwise. Smith wrote of how "the demand for men necessarily governs the production of men, as of every other commodity."[10] Marx would deplore, as Smith did, this degradation, but would not accept it as the necessary price for increased wealth. If Smith praises the landlord as serving the general interest of society (he sees the manufacturer and merchant as opposed to that interest), Marx will disagree and assert that, in any case, the landlord has become a capitalist, leaving only two parties—classes—in the economic world: capitalists and laborers.

It is in discussing alienated labor, however, that Marx directly moves away from Smith and his conception of economic theory to Feuerbach and positive criticism. Marx first raises the subject in passing, when he quotes Smith to the effect that "it is in the progressive state, while the society is advancing to the further acquisition, rather than when it has acquired its full complement of riches, that the condition of the laboring poor, of the great body of the people, seems to be the happiest and the most comfortable. It is hard in the stationary, and miserable in the declining state." Marx will have none of this, and insists that even in the favorable state the worker's lot is one of misery. He then comments that the growth of capital and revenues in a country are only possible "as the result of the accumulation of much labour, capital being accumulated labour; as the result, therefore, of the fact that his products are being taken in ever increasing degree from the hands of the worker, that to an increasing extent his own labour confronts him as another's property."

Smith wished to establish a rational science of economics, to be applied to the developments he saw occurring around him. Marx wished to work out a revolutionary philosophy, which would change Smith's world. Starting in the *Economic and Philosophic Manuscripts*, and most evident in the work to come, such as *The German Ideology*, and the *Manifesto* and *Capital*, Marx would stand Smith on his head, just as he was doing to Hegel, and use his economic science to ends unanticipated by the Scottish thinker. Marx, too, would claim a science; but it would be a science of man and history, eliminating Smith's economic science and the world it was describing. One can barely glimpse this development in the *Economic and Philosophical Manuscripts*, as it speaks of wages, profits, and rent; but it is emergent in Marx's concept of alienated labor.

Marx begins his discussion by asking a critical question of political economics. In starting from the fact of private property, does it not take "for granted what it is supposed to evolve?" In place of such a supposed fact, Marx will proceed "from an *actual* economic fact": the worker becomes "all the poorer the more wealth he produces." His increased poverty is not so much a decline in living standards—in fact, Marx insists that he is poorer even if better paid—as an increase in alienation: "The object which labour produces—labour's product—confronts it as *something alien. . .* " In short, the worker has become impoverished as a *human being*, through his own alienated labor; and, returning to his original question, Marx informs us that private property, it turns out, is the consequence, not the cause of alienated labor.

The concept of alienation was not new with Marx. Rousseau had spoken in romantic terms of man's alienation from nature and his natural self, as civilization developed. Hegel spoke of it as an ontological fact, i.e., one rooted in man's being, condemned as he was to be a self radically disassociated into actor and thing, subject and object. What Marx mainly added was that man's alienation originated in his work, or labor—Hegel had rooted it in action in general—and takes a number of forms: (1) man's labor becomes objectified in a product, which, no longer his own under capitalism, becomes an alien object dominating him; (2)

in the act of production itself, man is alienated—"emasculated"—from his own nature, becoming a cretin or machine; (3) he is estranged from other men; and (4) from his culture. In sum, from what Marx calls his species-being.

Marx's language and idea is highly philosophical—and speculative. He assures us, however, that "we took our departure from a fact of political economy—the estrangement of the worker and his production. We have formulated the concept of this fact—estranged, alienated labour. We have analyzed this concept—hence analyzing merely a fact of political economy." As fact, of course, it is purely empirical; or so Marx would have us believe. Having established this fact, Marx can then pass on to a defiant appeal for a return to man's humanity to man. The way, obviously, Marx tells us, is to eliminate private property, to emancipate the worker from his estranged product. In turn, such emancipation contains "universal human emancipation."

Communism is the end of private property. Marx distinguishes sharply between crude communism—the primitive notions of Cabet and others—whose only aim is community of women and goods at the most primitive, thoughtless level, and his own "*Communism* as the positive transcendence of private property, or human self-estrangement, and therefore as the real appropriation of the human essence by and for man; communism therefore as the complete return of man to himself as a social (i.e., human) being—a return become conscious, and accomplished within the entire wealth of previous development. This communism, as fully-developed naturalism, equals humanism, and as fully-developed humanism equals naturalism; it is the genuine resolution of the conflict between man and nature and between man and man—the true resolution of the strife between existence and essence, between objectification and self-confirmation, between freedom and necessity, between the individual and species." It is at the end of this last passage that Marx adds, "Communism is the riddle of history solved, and it knows itself to be this solution."

The prosaic thinker, such as John Stuart Mill, might think communism an economic system. For Marx, it is the "riddle of history solved," the return of man to himself. "In place of the *wealth* and *poverty* of political economy," he says, "come the rich *human* being and rich *human* need." Marx also believed that he was laying the ground work for "a psychology" which was "a genuine, comprehensive and *real* science." His own words, and his call for a real mental science, therefore, seem to point us to an attention to a real human being and his needs, to a psychology as well as a political economy of man.

Would such a real human being and psychology have anything to do with Marx as an actual, real, historical human being? Marx clearly spurned such an "egoistic" answer. He restricted his psychological analysis to such insights as that, often, political economy, the science of wealth, was simultaneously the "science of denial," i.e., he foreshadows Weber's theory of the Protestant Ethic and the Spirit of Capitalism.

Yet we dimly sense that Marx's own humanity and psychology speak through some of his seemingly "objective," philosophical, critical statements. For example, when Marx declares that, since for socialist man "the *entire so-called history of the world* is nothing but the begetting of man through human labour, nothing but the coming-to-be of nature for man, he has the visible, irrefutable proof of his birth through himself, of his process of coming-to-be," we tend to read this as an Hegelian notion, belonging simply to the realm of philosophy or ideology. It is that; but is it something else, as well? What does it mean when a serious thinker such as Marx also writes, a bit before this passage, "A *being* only considers himself independent when he stands on his own feet; and he only stands on his own feet when he owes his *existence* to himself. A man who lives by the grace of another regards himself as a dependent being. But I live completely by the grace of another if I owe him not only the sustenance of my life, but if he has, moreover, *created* my *life*—if he is the *source* of my life; and if it is not of my own creation, my life has necessarily a source of this kind outside it"? He then adds, "Self-generation . . . is the only practical refutation of the theory of creation."

Marx has told us that man makes religion, man makes his history, and now man makes himself. This is also the Marx who would confess to prizing strength above all other traits in man and to detesting servility most. Is he achieving a sense of total personal independence by claiming to have created himself? Or is he merely indulging in the vague, longing, and sometimes obfuscating language of Hegelian idealism? When Marx, at the end of the *Economic and Philosophic Manuscripts*, devotes two or three pages to analyzing "the Power of Money in Bourgeois Society" by excoriating money as "the *pimp* between man's need and the object" and the "common whore . . . of people and nations," is he merely gilding his economic analysis or encrusting it as well with feelings derived from his youthful relations to his father?

The answers are not obvious. In the case of religion, the connection is clearer. When Marx writes of the alienated product of labor first belonging to the gods (for example, the building of temples, etc.), before being appropriated by the capitalists, or speaks of money as the "visible divinity," we see the link of his economic critique to his religious critique; and behind the latter, we have glimpsed his personal religious experience. As the clouds of philosophy become thicker, taking on a life of their own, it is much more difficult to discern the Promethean figure whose fire brings them into being. The clouds seem almost self-created.

The *Economic and Philosophic Manuscripts* are not easy to read or understand in any terms. Much of their appeal rests on the "humanistic," almost poetic, quality that animates the sometimes dense, sometimes soaring, prose. "Assume *man* to be *man* and his relationship to the world to be a human one: then you can exchange love only for love, trust for trust, etc.," Marx writes in his final paragraph; and we, as readers, resonate to the aspirations therein voiced. "If you love without evoking love in return—that is, if your loving as loving does not produce reciprocal love; if through a living expression of yourself as a loving person you do not make yourself a loved person, then your love is impotent— a misfortune," Marx concludes, and we sigh empathically.

Surely, we feel, this is the way life ought to be. One should not be able to purchase love with money. Or the products of labor. "Marx with a Human face" promises us a better world. The Marx who, himself, was filled with so much hatred for his philistine enemies is lyrical about love. Self-love is attacked in the name of love of humanity. The world he wishes to create is a lovely one, and we feel uplifted by and to it. The only question remaining, for Marx, if not for us, is how we are to get to this new world. To answer that question, we must return to the present world, and to the proletariat who will bring about the final revolution, the last nodal point, in history.

VII

The Materialist
Interpretation
of History

There was little love in Marx's next work, *The Holy Family*, written in collaboration with Engels (in point of fact, Engels wrote only twelve pages). Oddly enough, where a number of more important and better written works were not published in Marx's life, this esoteric, polemical attack on Bauer and his followers, subsequently to be little read, was. Though a few of Marx's ideas on the materialist conception of history do peep through—there is, especially, an interesting section on French materialism—the book is not of much importance in this regard. *The German Ideology* is another story.

It was written in Brussels. Marx, as we saw, had been expelled from France in early 1845. Financially, the Marxes were relatively well off at this time, and Jenny, pregnant with Laura, was aided by the arrival of her own maid, Helene Demuth, or Lenchen. Engels also moved to Brussels, living next to the Marxes. It was a happy and productive time. In July, Marx and Engels took a six-week trip to England, spending most of the visit in Manchester, where they read up on the English economists. Back in Brussels, the two men began work on a book which would combine their new research with a criticism of Feuerbach.

As a preliminary to his break with Feuerbach—and we have noted it as part of a pattern, with Hegel and Bauer as predecessors—Marx had penned eleven "Theses on Feuerbach", which stands separate from *The*

German Ideology, in the spring. Now, in September 1845, a few months later, Marx and Engels sat down together finally "to settle accounts with our erstwhile philosophical conscience" and to write a complete work. It is only the first part of *The German Ideology* that is a critique of Feuerbach and is of major importance—the longer, second part is a critique of other Young Hegelians. None of the manuscript, in fact, found a publisher, and the authors ceased work on it in the fall of 1846. It was not published untill 1932. Marx accepted the failure to have the book published with equanimity; as he wrote later, "We abandoned the manuscript to the gnawing of the mice all the more willingly as we had achieved our main purpose—self-clarification." He was too modest: the theses of *The German Ideology* were to gnaw away at the foundations of capitalism.

Let us look first, however, at the preliminary work, the "Theses on Feuerbach," which was published in 1888, and only then as an appendage to Engels's *Ludwig Feuerbach and the End of Classical German Philosophy*. It was solely Marx's work.[1] Most of the eleven theses are short and aphoristic. The first one, however, is a long paragraph, and, announcing as it does Marx's redefinition of Feuerbach's materialism, deserves to be quoted at a whole:

> The chief defect of all hitherto existing materialism—that of Feuerbach included—is that the thing, reality, sensuousness, is conceived only in the form of the object or of *contemplation*, but not as *human sensuous activity*, *practice*, not subjectively. Hence it happened that the *active* side, in contradistinction to materialism, was developed by idealism—but only abstractly, since, of course, idealism does not know real, sensuous activity as such. Feuerbach wants sensuous objects, really distinct from the thought objects, but he does not conceive human activity itself as *objective* activity. Hence, in *Das Wesen des Christentums*, he regards the theoretical attitude as the only genuinely human attitude, while practice is conceived and fixed only in its dirty-judaical manifestation. Hence he does not grasp the significance of 'revolutionary', of practical-critical, activity.

Marx's genius was to fuse Hegel's "active" idealism with Feuerbach's "passive" materialism, metamorphosing the latter's abstraction into objective, practical—"dirty-judaical"—materialism. The result: a revolutionary explosion. Hegel's appeal for Marx is that he emphasizes man's creative powers, his activity in the world, his striving will, his Promethean strength. But Hegel is an idealist, for whom conflict occurs in terms of spirits. Feuerbach's appeal for Marx is that he dethrones the spirits and brings them down to earth, from whence they had originally been created by man. But Feuerbach, though a materialist, only deals with real, sensuous activity in idealistic, reified terms.

Marx goes beyond both. He is interested, as Feuerbach is not, in the "dirty-judaical" aspect of real life, as we have seen in the "Jewish Question." The "dirty-judaical" is the lurid way in which he refers to the economic world he had begun to study. It is the realm of civil society. Hegel had glimpsed that realm in idealistic terms; Marx would analyze it in materialistic terms—and then go beyond this realm in those same terms. As he remarks in thesis X, "The standpoint of the old materialism is 'civil' society; the standpoint of the new is *human* society, or socialized humanity."

There are other good things in the "Theses." In III, Marx points out that, though men are products of circumstances, "it is men who change circumstances," and then adds cryptically, "It is essential to educate the educator himself," without specifying who or what is to do the educating. In VI, he foreshadows an important part of his theory when he writes, "Feuerbach resolves the religious essence into the human essence. But the human essence is no abstraction inherent in each single individual. In its reality it is the ensemble of the social relations." Marx would spend much of the rest of his life and work analyzing "the ensemble of the social relations." His aim was not scholarly, but revolutionary. As his last, oft-quoted thesis, XI, announces, "The philosophers have only *interpreted* the world, in various ways; the point, however, is to *change* it." And change it he would.

The change Marx initiated, resulting in half the globe today following some variant of his ideas, was guided by his theories and, I would add, his dreams and wishes. It is easier, of course, to trace the former, and their development and form is especially evident in *The German Ideology*, where, seemingly at one bound, Marx has brought together the basic ideas which go to make up his mature concept of the materialistic nature of history.[2]

Marx (and Engels) begins by satirizing the Young Hegelians, his former companions, for their "dependence on Hegel," which makes their allegedly "world-shattering" statements actually hollow and conservative. Marx, it is clear, is claiming his independence from the father of them all, Hegel. The problem with the Young Hegelians, Marx declares, is that they have not inquired into the connection of German philosophy with German reality, i.e., the relation of their own thought to their own material circumstances.

Unlike the servile disciples of Hegel, Marx will start from premises that are not arbitrary, but real: real individuals and real activities. These premises, he insists, can "be verified in a purely empirical way." The first premise of history must be that men exist, i.e., produce means of subsistence, which allow them to go on living. Such physical existence of the individual is reproduced in a particular mode of production. The mode itself reflects the degree of division of labor, which is a measure of "how far the productive forces of a nation are developed." The stages of development in the division of labor also mark the different forms of ownership, and Marx identifies three: (1) the tribal; (2) the ancient communal and State ownership, based on union of several tribes into a city, or *polis*; and (3) the feudal, or "estate property."

Here we have the future schema or periodization of history, which Marx will always use henceforth (adding an Asiatic period) and develop in rich detail especially in the work called *Grundrisse*. It is hardly a novel schema. Starting with the tribal, it moves to ancient, medieval, and, to be added, modern history. The same stages are to be found in Hegel and numerous others. What is novel is the way in which Marx links the stages to material production, division of labor, and ownership of property, and then reifies the "actual" history into a general theory of social development.

He was clearly proud of his breakthrough to "real, positive science." He claims that "In direct contrast to German philosophy which descends from heaven to earth, here we ascend from earth to heaven." Ideas, he goes on, or conceptions, in short, consciousness, are the result of material circumstances, not pure Reason. Men "are the producers of their conceptions, ideas, etc.—real, active men as they are conditioned by a definite development of their productive forces." The idealists only see ideologically, i.e., in an inverted or upside-down fashion, "as in a *camera obscura*," their inverted vision arising "just as much from their historical life-process as the inversion of objects on the retina does from their physical life-process." Triumphantly, Marx declares, "The phantoms formed in the human brain are also, necessarily, sublimates of their material life-process, which is empirically verifiable and bound to material premises."

Others have only ideology; Marx has real, positive, empirically verifiable science. With the depiction of reality, philosophy as an independent branch of knowledge is at an end, he announces. We see here, as if illuminated by a bolt of lightening linking heaven and earth, the movement of Marx's thought from and through humanism to scientific socialism. He has broken through to a new stage of his own development and his theory's development all at once. It is almost as if he were still gasping at his effort, for immediately he returns to the beginning and once again goes over in more detail his initial premises.

To "make history," Marx reminds us, men must first live, and life requires the production of means to satisfy needs. Satisfaction of one need leads to new needs, "and this production of new needs is the first historical act." Men must also make other men, i.e., propagate (Marx has no trouble using "men" in a generic sense). All these forms of production have a double aspect: they are a natural and also a social, i.e., cooperative, relationship. Marx is now spelling out the "ensemble of the social relations" mentioned in VI of his "Theses on Feuerbach."

It follows, Marx goes on, "that a certain mode of production, or industrial stage, is always combined with a certain mode of co-operation, or social stage, and this mode of co-operation is itself a 'productive force'." Credit must be given the French and the English for first grasping that history must be written with a materialistic basis; they were the first, he tells us, to write histories of civil society, of commerce and industry. Marx builds on their theoretical work, just as he incorporates the actual work, i.e., production, of the bourgeoisie in his own theories, and incorporates their ideas into his own analysis of the "social ensemble." The multitude of productive forces, he continues, "determines the nature of society, hence . . . the 'history of humanity' must always be studied and treated in relation to the history of industry and exchange." Such a history, he concludes, would proceed independent "of the existence of any political or religious nonsense which would especially hold men together."

Inspired by such convictions, Marx became a premier historian of capitalism. He made economic history central to his theoretical work. It is the "empirical" side of Marx's future writings. We must note that his theory does not grow out of a study of economic history, but rather leads to the latter. Economic history, for Marx, becomes a confirmation "after the fact" of critical analysis. We must also note that Marx is dismissing political history—and political life—as "nonsense." There is, to take one example, no social contract à la Rousseau to be assumed or worried about; only economic—productive—relations tie man to man in a fundamental sense. Such a view marks a profound revolution in political science.

Marx, of course, was aware that men had ideas. But these were as much a matter of "production" as were material goods and life. Indeed, ideas arose out of and were determined by the material conditions of production. "Consciousness" is the term Marx uses for man's ideational life, and he declares that "Consciousness is . . . from the very beginning a social product." At this point, Marx diverts his argument from a further discussion of what we now call the "sociology of knowledge"—a profound, even if partial, insight into the social nature of epistemology—and comments on the division of labor.

In the beginning, consciousness is only "herd-consciousness." Increased productivity, needs, and population—and we have already seen Marx's discussion of these essentials to the making of history—lead inexorably to the development of the division of labor. (I have always been stunned by what Marx says next, that the division of labor "was originally nothing but the division of labour in the sexual act"; my shock comes from his later desire to eliminate the division of labor.)* The division then, historically, becomes one between material and mental labor; and it is this division that allows the illusion that consciousness is somehow independent from the real conditions of production.

Such division also leads to the fact that "enjoyment and labour, production and consumption—devolve on different individuals." Hence, we also have unequal distribution, both qualitatively and quantitatively, of labor and its products; thus, property. Division of labor, Marx insists, and private property are "identical expressions." As long as division of labor is not voluntarily chosen, "man's own deed becomes an alien power opposed to him, which enslaves him instead of being controlled by him."

Adam Smith saw in the division of labor the source of man's in-

---

* Worthy of note is the fact that William Godwin, in his *Enquiry Concerning Political Justice* (1793) foresaw a society in which people, become cultivated and virtuous, would "probably cease to propagate". In his utopia, "The whole will be a people of men, and not of children. Generation will not succeed generation, nor truth have, in a certain degree, to recommence her career every thirty years. . . . There will be no wars, no crimes, no administration of justice, as it is called, and no government. Beside this, there will be neither disease, anguish, melancholy, nor resentment. Every man will seek, with ineffable ardour, the good of all." The reader can make his own comparison with Marx's longed for society; Godwin also suggested that human life would be prolonged "beyond any limits which we are able to assign", i.e., to a kind of immortality. Such an idea is entirely missing in Marx.[3]

creased productivity and thus his growing affluence. For Marx, it is the source of alienation. With division of labor, each man's activity is forced into an exclusive sphere—does the Marx who agonized over his choice of a vocation, and fluctuated between different careers, speak with special feeling here? Man in such circumstances, Marx continues, is a hunter, a fisherman, a shepherd, or a critical critic, and must remain so if he wishes to assure his livelihood. Only in communist society will society regulate the general productivity and thus make it possible, as Marx lyrically puts it, "for me to do one thing today and another tomorrow, to hunt in the morning, fish in the afternoon, rear cattle in the evening, criticize after dinner, just as I have in mind, without ever becoming hunter, fisherman, shepherd or critic." It is a *cri de coeur* of every youth of imagination.

Marx, of course, had predecessors in this longing. Charles Fourier, whom Marx may well have read, outlines a typical day in his phalanstery, listing an individual's activity at every hour. I excerpt a few entries: "at 5 ½ . . . a session in a hunting group"; "at 7 . . . a session in a fishing group"; and so on.[4]

The paradox is that, in historically existing societies until now, it is in the laissez-faire system that we see the closest approximation to the individual choosing his own job—what he will do. Economic necessity, of course, constrains most workers to accept certain types of labor, under a time discipline not their own, often in an exploitive situation, and within a framework of division of labor. Yet, in comparison with a "command," or communist, economy, where the individual is assigned his job (what, I wonder, would have happened to Marx?)—e.g., Communist China—a capitalist economy allows a certain latitude to some people in the way they will spend their "working " day. Marx, as we know, wished to go beyond both a capitalist and a command economy; the question is whether, for the foreseeable future, his wish is utopian.

The millennial strain in Marx emerges powerfully right here. It may seem a contradiction in terms to view Marx, an atheist, as a millennialist. The same problem emerges in thinking of one of Marx's predecessors, whom he labeled a "utopian socialist," Robert Owen. Yet, as W. H. Oliver reminds us, "In religion, Robert Owen was both a deist and a millennialist, a child of the Enlightenment and an example of enthusiasm. Conventional views of eighteenth- and early nineteenth-century religion and irreligion do not easily accomodate these antitheses. We are used to a pattern which contrasts cool rationalist deists

with unstable enthusiasts, locating millennialists at the extreme of in-
stability and irrationality."[5] Marx, I am arguing, though atheist rather
than deist, straddles the division, just as does Robert Owen.

Marx was always vague about what his future society would really be
like—"sufficient unto the day are the problems we have" might be his
justifiable motto. Yet, he clearly had idyllic visions beckoning him—
and us—onwards. They were, as Lewis Feuer points out, shared with
Engels who wrote to him in October, 1844, that communism already
existed in certain American communities:

> The Germans are all still unclear concerning the actual practicability of
> communism; to put an end to this rubbish, I shall write a small brochure
> to show that the project has already been realized, and to depict in a pop-
> ular fashion the existing practice of communism in England and America.
> It will cost me three days or so, and will clear things up for the yokels very
> much.[6]

Engels was referring primarily to several American religious communities: the Shakers, the Harmonizers, and the Separatists.

The Shakers, especially, attracted Engels' admiration: they enjoyed
community of property, yet were hard-working though apparently free
to choose what they wished to work at; they had no political structure,
i.e., police, judges, laws, and so forth. He notes their strange custom
of prohibiting both marriage and sexual intercourse—shades of Godwin
and of Marx's comment on the division of labor!—but ascribes little importance to it. (Engels, incidentally, was a notorious womanizer.) Similarly, he observes the religious foundations of all his communist communities, but draws no inference from this fact, nor from the further
fact that the Harmonizers, for example, functioned effectively because
they were under the political dictatorship of their leader, Rapp.

By the time of *The Communist Manifesto*, both Marx and Engels would
change their minds about the "rubbish." In a pattern we are now familiar with, they ridiculed those who wished "to march straightway into
the social New Jerusalem," and dismissed as ineffectual those who "still
dream of experimental realization of their social utopias, of founding
isolated '*phalansteries.*' "

From 1844 to 1848 Marx had worked forward to his materialist interpretation, as I am now trying to make manifest. I do not believe he had
abjured or relinquished his millennial, utopian dream—it is the psychic

drive behind what came to be Marxism—but to it he has added the "scientific" analysis of existing capitalist society, an analysis which, with all its weaknesses, is still one of the most powerful aids that we have to understand our present society. It is obtuse, however, not to distinguish conceptually between these two aspects of Marx's work, even though they developed together and are cognitively joined in one man, Marx.

We need to return to *The German Ideology* itself as this point. For Marx, division of labor also underlies the emergence of the State. The latter is an illusory communal life, though based on the real ties of family, language, and especially class, and "it follows from this that all struggles within the State, the struggle between democracy, aristocracy, and monarchy, the struggle for the franchise, etc., etc., are merely the illusory forms in which the real struggles of the different classes are fought out among one another." Struggles in, and among states—political life, in short—therefore, is only a veil for the real struggles based on the division of labor and private property, which are, with all that is built upon them, the basis of man's estrangement from himself and what he produces. They will be abolished when the development of the material conditions of life have (1) rendered the great mass of humanity propertyless, and (2) reached a high level of productivity in society at large. As one instance of what he has in mind, Marx notes that "slavery cannot be abolished without the steam engine and the mule and spinning-jenny, serfdom cannot be abolished without improved agriculture."

Such a development of productive forces and class alignment, moreover, must be on a world-historical scale. "Empirically," Marx declares, "communism is only possible as the act of the dominant peoples 'all at once' and simultaneously, which presupposes the universal development of productive forces and the world intercourse bound up with communism." The proletariat must become a world-historical hero; and will so become. For communism is not a mere ideal, but a "*real* movement which abolishes the present state of things."

At this point, Marx has in place the fundamentals of his materialist conception of history and communism. The rest is elaboration. But, oh, what dramatic elaboration of the basic plot! And, as I shall discuss later, what effort at a social science! At this point, however, Marx's argument in *his* text takes a different turn. Rather than pursuing here the elaboration of his efforts at a social science, he has more immediate polemical aims in mind. "Saint Bruno" and "Blessed Max Stirner" (author of *The Ego and His Own*, viewed by Marx as an anarchistic, self-indulgent book) first need the halos knocked off them. "High-falutin and haughty hucksters of ideas," Marx calls them. He also accuses Bauer of being parochially German, oblivious of world history. Feuerbach, too, gets his lumps: Marx describes his erstwhile esteemed mentor as "grossly . . . deceiving himself."

Mixed with the polemic are, nevertheless, other gems of Marxist analysis and prose. As Marx states, forms and products of consciousness cannot be dissolved by mental criticism as such; they are overthrown by practical transformations of the actual social relations. "Not criticism but revolution," he repeats, "is the driving force of history." And revolution is brought about by real men, in real productive relations, which are changing. Feuerbach had stopped at the abstraction "man." Marx, forgetting, or not mentioning, his own encomium in the *Economic and Philosophic Manuscripts*, is scornful of Feuerbach, who "knows no other 'human relationships' 'of man to man' than love to friendship, and even then idealised." So much, it appears, for the humanist Marx! He has turned for the moment, at least implicitly, his own face against his earlier being.

The gain is in analytic power, though always driven, and possibly distorted, or over-simplified, by the revolutionary intent. In a now famous quote, Marx goes on: "The ideas of the ruling class are in every epoch the ruling ideas: i.e., the class which is the ruling *material* force of society, is at the same time its ruling *intellectual* force." Then follows a further elaboration of this idea; and the way in which the modern ruling class, the bourgeoisie, came to power. Thus, Marx discusses the separation of town and country consequent upon the division of labor, the development of the burgher class in the Middle Ages, and its rise to supremacy in the 17th and 18th centuries, especially in England. The result is universal competition, industrial cities—and the bourgeois form of production now itself becoming a constraint on further development: the development of bourgeois capitalism "produced a mass of productive forces, for which private [property] became just as much a fetter as the guild had been for manufacture. . . ."**

The "fetter" will be broken by a revolution. The next stage of consciousness itself will be a by-product rather than a cause of that revolution, or, rather, will develop along with it. In Marx's words: "Both for

** It is worth noting here that the imagery of "chains," as in Rousseau's *Social Contract*, has given way to that of "fetters," marking the shift from a primarily politically based servitude to an economic one.

the production on a mass scale of this communist consciousness, and for the success of the cause itself, the alteration of men on a mass scale is necessary, an alteration which can only take place in a practical movement, a *revolution*; this revolution is necessary, therefore, not only because the *ruling* class cannot be overthrown in any other way, but also because the class *overthrowing* it can only in a revolution succeed in ridding itself of all the muck of ages and become fitted to found society anew." It is only in the activity of revolution itself that man makes himself into a new man, cleansed and purified. With such statements, Marx himself, finally reached in *The German Ideology*, as he would see it, his intellectual manhood. The fundamental elements of the so-called "mature" or "old" Marx are to be found here. Whatever their later development, we are now in possession of his total theory (with the possible exception of the theory of surplus value, a different kind of theory). It is a broad and encompassing one. His theories about ideology and consciousness, ruling classes, economic determinism, and the development of proletarian revolution are all brought together in one overall vision. His connection of the division of labor, private property, and the state, and his call for their simultaneous abolitions are put before us in one arching synthesis.

So to speak, Marx has "unfettered" himself intellectually. He would maintain that he had broken the ties binding him to Hegel, Bauer, Feuerbach. In fact, our study suggests a continuity as well as a transcendence. Humanism and the new social science are connected by Marx's own human needs, aspirations, and development. The putative science has emerged from critical philosophy, critical philosophy from critical religion, and all from Marx, the man, striving to fulfill his vocation and to be a new man in circumstances of his own choosing.

Marx had said, "It is men who change circumstances." By willful activity, Marx's ambition was to create a new world, based on the destruction of an old one. He wished a revolution. By his revolution, he envisaged the creation of circumstances which would be communistic. Here, at the end of days, for the proletariat revolution is the last, communism would institute a set of circumstances that would no longer fetter man or society, letting both exist out of time, free. By 1846 and *The German Ideology*, Marx felt he had established scientific verification of this future of man; in the end, will had become transfigured into necessity.[7]

II

The *Communist Manifesto* of 1848 was the herald of the coming revolution.[8] The American Revolution of 1776 and the French Revolution of 1789 did not issue manifestos but rather declarations. The Declaration of Independence and the Declaration of Rights of Man and the Citizen were written *after* revolution had started; they were *ex post facto* statements as to the grounds of rebellion and the rights asserted in the revolution. Marx's manifesto was of a different nature.

Where the declarations spoke of self-evident, static rights of Man, the Manifesto talked of a logic of history, dialectically establishing the existence and "rights" of the proletariat; where they spoke of timeless Man, it talked of historical classes; where they justified a national revolution—American or French—it established the claims of an international revolution; where they defended present gains it predicted a future upheaval.

Marx drew his inspiration from the French Revolution, but from a different strand than that of the "bourgeois" declarations. After the Reign of Terror came Thermidor in the the French Revolution. By 1795, a Directory was in power, and the Revolution had turned conservative, i.e., it was consolidating its revolutionary gains. Some saw this development as a betrayal of the Revolution, and plotted the overturn of the Directory and its bourgeois republic. Men such as Gracchus Babeuf and Sylvain Maréchal formed a Conspiracy of Equals and secretly planned a coup d'etat. Publicly, they issued a "Manifesto of the Equals." Penetrated by the police, the conspiracy was broken up, its leaders arrested, and Babeuf executed.

Its conspiratorial and "communistic" mantle was taken up, however, by new revolutionaries, such as Blanqui and Buonarroti. Such men kept alive; during the first part of the 19th century, the tradition of a permanent revolution, i.e., a continuation of the French Revolution.[9] They became professional revolutionaries. In an age of increasing specialization, they, too, devoted their whole lives to one craft or vocation: revolution. (I have called some members of this group "revolutionary ascetics".) Small in number, they formed secret societies—it was a time of secret societies, such as the Free Masons or the Carbonaris, with their esoteric symbols, hand shakes, and rites—and dreamed their dreams and plotted their plots of revewed revolution.

The "League of the Just," as we have seen, was formed in 1836 by

German radical workers living in Paris; it drew upon this heritage. It, too, was secret and small in number; and it aimed at a revolution in Germany that would establish a "social" republic, as well as the Rights of Man and the Citizen. After the failure of a Blanquist uprising in 1839, the majority of its members left Paris for London, where, in 1847, the name was changed to "Communist League." Its beliefs had fluctuated from faith in a Blanquist *putsch* to the peaceful utopian communism of Etienne Cabet, from conspiracy to conversion. The League felt it was time to proclaim their views openly to an expectant world, though they necessarily remained a secret society.

At its annual congress in late 1847, the League commissioned Marx and Engels, who had only recently joined the group, to draft a manifesto of its aims. The League itself was riven by factions, and thus unsure itself of what direction—radical or restrained, communistic or democratic—it should go, and this fact is partly reflected in the *Manifesto* itself.

Engels prepared a draft, "Principles of Communism," which was a catechism of twenty-five questions and answers. He wisely wrote Marx, however, "Think over the confession of faith a bit. I think it would be better to drop the catechistic form and call the thing a communist manifesto."[10] Engels' language of "faith" is significant (later, he was to call *Capital* "The Worker's Bible"). He also recommended the bringing in of a certain amount of history. Such advice fell on willing and prepared ears. Marx was aware that he had found the vehicle to proclaim to the world in simple and dramatic terms the scientific revelation about man and society he had worked out in *The German Ideology*. He set to work to impose his vision on the document. As we have seen Engels acknowledge, "The basic thought running through the Manifesto . . . belongs solely and exclusively to Marx."[11] In fact, Marx did all the actual writing. It is the power of his prose, the impassioned drama of his "science," that makes the *Manifesto* a classic document and one of the great "confessions of faith."

Marx begins by an act of hyperbole: "A spectre is haunting Europe— the spectre of Communism." This is magnificent propaganda. The fact was that the Communists were only a handful of sectarians—the League in London numbered variously fifteen to twenty to one hundred members—a gadfly at best to the reactionary European Powers. Marx, however, makes them the only alternate to the status quo. He establishes this Manichean dualism by the simple device of assertion: "Communism is already acknowledged by all European Powers to be itself a Power." It is high time, therefore, that "Communists should openly, in the face of the whole world, publish their views . . . and meet this nursery tale of the Spectre of Communism with a Manifesto of the party itself."

The rest is history, although the *Manifesto* had to wait sixty-nine years for *its* revolution. Marx's materialist interpretation of history is outlined in the first two sections: "Bourgeoisie and Proletarians" and "Proletarians and Communists." Marx, the gravedigger of the bourgeoisie, is most lyrical in his funeral oration. His encomiums of the bourgeoisie—of capitalism—are unsurpassed. After all, they have, historically, "played a most revolutionary part." It is worth quoting the whole of Marx's tribute:

> The bourgeoisie, during its rule of scarce one hundred years, has created more massive and more colossal productive forces than have all preceding generations together. Subjection of Nature's forces to man, machinery, application of chemistry to industry and agriculture, steam-navigation, railways, electric telegraphs, clearing of whole continents for cultivation, canalisation of rivers, whole populations conjured out of the ground—what earlier century had even a presentiment that such productive forces slumbered in the lap of social labour?

In the framework of historical necessity the bourgeoisie *must* play a revolutionary role, in order to bring the proletariat into existence and to prepare the conditions, or circumstances, for *its* revolution. Indeed, we have seen Marx's annoyance and disappointment at the failure of the bourgeois to play their revolutionary part in Germany during the 1840s. On a world stage, however, they were more heroic thespians.

The problem is that, though Marx needs to praise the bourgeois for their heroic role, he must also disparage them as the villains they must become in the next, and final, act. He pulls this feat off by his masterful writing style. The familar sounds of Marx's prose resound in our ears. "The bourgeoisie," he tells us, "wherever it has got the upper hand, has put an end to all feudal, patriarchal, idyllic relations. It has pitilessly torn asunder the motley feudal ties that bound man to his 'natural superiors,' and has left remaining no other nexus between man and man than naked self-interest, than callous 'cash payment.' " Does Marx really believe feudal relations were "idyllic"? Of course not. He is satirizing the feudal relations *at the same time* as he is deprecating the bourgeois, *even while* his own interpretation of history requires him to praise them for their revolutionary role. Analysis only requires him to state that the bourgeoisie has dissolved the feudal ties, as an historical fact; revolutionary fervor impels him to say "pitilessly torn asunder" and to add the word "callous" to Thomas Carlyle's earlier invention of the phrase, "cash payment" and "cash nexus."[12]

Marx, as we have seen, was a trenchant and sometimes savage critic of religion. Yet his choice of words chastises the bourgeoisie for having "drowned the most heavenly ecstasies of religious fervour . . . in the icy water of egotistical calculation." How would Marx describe his own critique?

Another example: "The bourgeoisie has torn away from the family its sentimental veil, and has reduced the family relation to a mere money relation." Here we must pause. There are two problems with Marx's formulation about the family. The first is that the bourgeois family, as a matter of historical fact, *lost* its economic significance in large part and *gained* a heightened affective quality, i.e., became a "haven in a heartless world." Romantic love appeared. At the very least, romantic love was a weapon wielded by the bourgeoisie against the aristocracy—one thinks of "The Marriage of Figaro" and "Clarissa"—at the same time that it was turned against the bourgeoisie itself, as its children married for love, not money.

The second problem is psychological: after, if not before, his father's death, Marx certainly reduced his natal family relation to a mere money relation, even if he preserved affective ties within his own marriage. Further, his accusations, as we have noted, about the bourgeoisie taking the leading role in prostitution—"having the wives and daughters of their proletarians at their disposal"—as well as taking "the greatest pleasure in seducing each other's wives," is also troubling in terms of his own behavior.

Rather than diverting his readers from his main message, however, Marx's animadversions on such subjects were merely titillating. Only a careful reader would be distracted from the grand sweep of his historical dialectic, which told how the bourgeoisie rose in opposition to the feudal aristocracy, revolutionized the instruments of production and thereby the relations of production, constantly expanded the market and created a world civilization, and stripped all occupations, institutions, and relations of their halos. In Marx's words, "All that is solid melts into air, all that is holy is profaned, and man is at last compelled to face with sober senses, his real conditions of life, and his relations with his kind."

The bourgeoisie has also created the conditions of its own doom. "Not only," Marx intoned, "has the bourgeoisie forged the weapons that bring death to itself; it has also called into existence the men who are to wield those weapons—the modern working class—the proletarians." The bourgeoisie has simplified the class struggle, which Marx claims to be "the history of all existing society," into a final Manichean struggle of only two classes: the haves and the have-nots, the capitalists and the proletarians. Marx then traces in some detail the development of the proletariat and its inevitable collision with and victory over the bourgeoisie. The bourgeoisie has necessarily produced its "own grave-diggers," and "its fall and the victory of the proletariat are equally inevitable." As the one class that is oppressed but cannot become an oppressor—the proletariat is identical "with the interests of the immense majority"—the proletariat's triumph will end the class struggle, and thus all hitherto existing history.

We can move quickly over the rest of the *Manifesto*. The role of the Communists is not to be a separate party opposed to other working-class parties, but to be identical with the interests of the proletariat as a whole. Such a role permits the Communists to be opportunistic. Marx was responding to the sectarian pressures and splits of the actual League when he wrote that in France the Communists ally themselves with the Social Democrats, in Switzerland with the Radicals, and in Germany with the bourgeoisie; but he was also responding to his own sense of historical development. He accepts the reproach that the desire to abolish private property is essential to Communism, but retorts that the abolition of existing property relations, e.g., the feudal, by the bourgeoisie is not new in history, and then excoriates the bourgeoisie for having already abolished private property for the proletariat, the immense majority of society. It is bourgeois property only that the Communists, consequently, have as their task to abolish.

As for practical, immediate measures, aside from the abolition of property in land and right of inheritance, Marx's list hardly seems too radical today: a heavy progressive or graduated income tax; centralization of credit in the hands of the State; same for communication and transport; bringing wastelands into cultivation, and the improvement of the soil generally in accordance with a common plan; combination of agriculture with manufacturing industries; and free education of all children in public schools. Equal liability of all to labor is not found in the United States today, but establishment of industrial armies, especially for agriculture, was temporarily tried in the Civilian Conservation Corps of the New Deal, and service in the military army is an equal liability.

These measures and other local, time-bound subjects, and Marx's own sectarian arguments against other Socialists—e.g., Feudal; Petty-Bourgeois; German, or 'True'; Conservative, or Bourgeois; and Critical-Utopian Socialists—are not what is remembered from the *Manifesto*. It is, rather, his stirring exposition of the historical drama, as it moves materialistically from the feudal aristocracy, to the bourgeoisie, and then to the proletariat and their triumph, which hums in our ears and is imprinted on our minds. "WORKING MEN OF ALL COUNTRIES, UNITE!", he trumpets at the end. "Let the ruling classes tremble at a Communistic revolution. The proletarians have nothing to lose but their chains. They have a world to win." It is a world which is humanly attractive. As Marx describes it, "In place of the old bourgeois society, with classes and class antagonisms, we shall have an association, in which the free development of each is the condition for the free development of all."

III

The *Manifesto* announces to the world the mature Marx. It made the Marx of his "theological" writings, with their endless splitting of hairs, into the Marx of mass appeal. The rest is, more or less, Epilogue.

I am by no means dismissing the remainder of Marx's life and work. (Indeed, I will devote the next chapter to *Capital* and to Marx's achievements as a social analyst.) It is filled with accomplishment. What I am saying is that by 1848 the fundamentals of Marx's intellectual and revolutionary creativity are in place—the "young" and "old" Marx have met; after the mid-century we encounter mainly elaborations.

We have already discussed briefly Marx's involvement with the revolution of 1848 and his scurrying back and forth between Paris and Cologne, editing periodicals, arming workers, and fighting trial battles. He continued to hope for a revolutionay outbreak, while more realistically realizing that it was too early for such a proletariat uprising: the bourgeoisie had to be given more years to nurture conditions in the womb of time. Meanwhile, Marx, in the British Museum, would study and write about the way the revolution would eventually have to come about, and inform the workers about the consciousness they must acquire.

He did not rest with theory; as we know, theory itself was merely a form of action, to be eventually abolished by the latter. Marx, therefore, also remained active. His was a mixture of realism and utopianism in both his theories and his actions. He changed his mind in both areas with some frequency. We have already seen his shifts from Hegel to Bauer to Feuerbach, and beyond; we might also note his on-again, off-again relations with collaborators such as Hess, Ruge, and Lassalle (though not Engels); and we could observe his changes in tactics, from secret to open, from dictatorial to democratic, in regard to the worker's movement.

Marx, for the rest of his life after 1850, was an émigré; and he immersed himself in London in émigré politics. They are the worst kind of politics: petty, suspicious, and vituperative, whether Bourbon in the early 19th century or Central American in the late 20th century. They called forth the worst in Marx. He jockeyed for power with the others, and wasted inordinate amounts of time in doing so. One vitriolic exchange, *Herr Vogt*, consumed eighteen months, much of his precious writing time, and a good deal of his money—to no ostensible purpose. Marx, unfortunately, was a good hater, willing to pursue his hates to the bitter end that seemed never to come.

He was also, as noted, a prodigious worker. Out of the sectarian, émigré quarrels, he (and Engels) did manage to impose, even if uneasily and ephemerally, his message and leadership on the feisty, splintered labor movement in London. In 1864, the International Working Men's Association was founded, with Marx as its guiding light. His leadership, however, was not unchallenged, and to avoid the loss of the International to Bakunin and the Proudhonists, he oversaw its effective dissolution in 1872, and its formal demise in 1875–76.[13] Still, he had imprinted his personality and thoughts on the First International, which was to be succeeded by a Second (1889–1914) and a Third (1919–1943), which came into being as the result, finally, of a Communist revolution, the Bolshevik Revolution.

It was Marx's writing, of course, which was his greatest achievement, and which was the means by which he came to dominate the revolutionary movement. He never ceased to be a journalist, even if he relegated it as a career to a secondary position and never earned a real living from it. For example, Marx published 487 articles in the *New York*

Tribune alone, of which 350 were his, 125 written by Engels, and twelve written in collaboration. Some of these articles were of a very high order (see, for example, "The British in India"), equal to the best of Marx's work, but he himself deprecated his journalism: "The continual newspaper muck annoys me. It takes a lot of time, disperses my efforts and in the final analysis is nothing. However independent one wishes to be, one is still dependent on the paper and its public especially if, as I do, one receives cash payment. Purely scientific works are something completely different. . . "[14]

Marx had a hard time ever completing any of his "scientific works." His intended grand opus on "Economics" petered out during 1857–58 into an unpublished, though posthumously impressive, *Grundrisse* (or "Foundations of a Critique of Political Economy," the title given to it by its editors in 1939–41); the *Contribution to the Critique of Political Economy*, which, finally appearing in 1859, was fragmentary and unsuccessful (only its Introduction is *echt Marx*); and *Capital* (1867) itself, which was only one-third finished when Marx died; Engels published the second and third volumes from Marx's posthumous notes.

Of course, there were also the semi-journalistic, semi-scientific works that were the "empirical" applications of Marx's "scientific" theories: "The Class Struggles in France, 1848–50," "The Eighteenth Brumaire of Louis Bonaparte," "The Civil War in France," and others, as well as innumerable letters, addresses, and circulars, in which Marx both exerted his authority over the working class movement and filled in lacunae in his theories and their applications.

All of these works, and especially *Capital*, were of great importance in giving substance and weight to Marx's ideas. They form the canon of faith for Marxists. They often offer brilliant contributions to the history and interpretation of 19th-century politics and of capitalist economic development. They are the fulfillment of the Marx who, though he died in 1883 at age sixty-five, came to full maturity in his early thirties. They are the exemplification of his "scientific humanism" already on display in such works as *The German Ideology* and *The Communist Manifesto*. They do not change, however, except in minor details, our understanding of Marx and his thought. If we want to comprehend and evaluate him and his work best, we do so in terms of the "young" Marx, who, as his followers realized, was already an "old" man in his thirties.

Hegel had spoken of "silent revolutions" in history. Marx, by his writings, brought into being such a revolution, which started with his critiques of the 1840s, worked largely underground in the rest of the 19th century (*Capital* was almost completely ignored on its appearance in 1867), smoldered openly in the social democratic politics of the late 19th–early 20th century, and burst into explosive force in 1917. The fallout is still with us. To use phrasing that would have been congenial to Marx himself, he had succeeded in being a "revolutionary scientist" as well as a "scientific revolutionist," with the "dynamite"—in this case, dynamic theory—having been invented and prepared by him during the failed revolution of 1848 and stored in *The Communist Manifesto*.

VIII

The Mystery of
Capital

Capital is Marx's most serious attempt at formal social science. It is high time that I deal with this "spectre," grown into a seven-hundred-page claim to scientific analysis (not to mention the two posthumous volumes). There is no question that it is a great work—though I disagree with one scholar that it is the "greatest work of nineteenth century thought" (what of *The Origin of Species?*). The question is whether it is a great "scientific" work, and in what sense. Robert Wolff, just quoted, also writes that "if Marx has any claim at all to lasting fame, it is as an economist."[1] As an economic work, in fact, *Capital* has run into serious trouble among most economists except those who specifically style themselves Marxist, and it has been more or less dismissed as a serious work of "science." Is this, however, a correct evaluation? (In the last twenty years, a number of younger professional economists have begun to take Marx more seriously, but to what effect it is not yet clear.)

First, let us look at Marx's leading ideas in *Capital* (specifically Volume I). Ideally, we would do so in terms of a close, critical analysis of the full text—as I have done with Marx's earlier writings—but there are two reasons for not doing this: (1) it would take a whole, new book; and (2) it is, for my purposes, unnecessary, for reasons I stated earlier in my arguments about the "young" and "old" Marx. Thus, I will treat *Capital* relatively briefly and with limited aims in mind.

Marx's economics is really a "science" within a "science." The larger science is the materialist interpretation of history. It is an historical science, which explains the evolution of human society, its "human technology." The dialectic of Marx's historical science explains how every past stage of society, as well as capitalism, has come into being, as well as how it will go out of existence. *Capital* is to explain the laws—economic laws, i.e., the lesser "science"—which operate in detail, in the capitalist system *per se*, and to demonstrate both how capitalism functions and how it will bring about its own destruction.

Marx assumes that classical economic theory, *suitably critiqued*, is, in fact, a "science" (as its founders claim), which can be relied upon. The mistake of Smith, Ricardo, and their like, in Marx's view, was to assume that the limited theory they offer is descriptive of the world as a whole, i.e., that their theories describe the objective process of laws which regulate and govern the relations between things in *any* society, rather than merely in capitalist society. They mistake for a general theory what is only a particular case. I agree with this view.

The leading ideas in *Capital* revolve around (1) a labor theory of value, (2) a theory of surplus value, (3) theories of capital accumulation, and (4) a law of increased misery. The labor theory of value was provided Marx by Adam Smith, as we have seen in relation to the *Economic and Philosophic Manuscripts*, and had became a commonplace by the mid-19th century. As such, it was a great intellectual achievement, for what Smith had done was to replace gold and silver, in mercantilism, or land, in physiocracy, with labor as the source of the wealth of nations. It might make sense to call Smith's theory "laborism" rather than capitalism. In a kind of Copernican revolution in economics, labor also became the *measure* of value: a commodity's value was the amount of labor required to produce it (confusion arose as to whether it really was the amount of labor the commodity could purchase). Marx, in basing *Capital* on the labor theory of value, was thus at the forefront of the economic science of his day.

Hard science, however, granting economics to be one for the moment, is supposed to change in its theory, as new data and logical problems arise. Marx had the misfortune to write *Capital* just before another revolution swept over economics: marginal utility theory. In the 1870s, Jevons in England, Walras in France, and Menger in Austria all worked out in increasingly mathematical terms a destructive criticism of the labor theory of value (presumably one that Marx, good critic as he was, might have welcomed). This is one of the reasons why modern, neo-classical economists pay little attention to Marx's work as anything more than an historical contribution to or curio in the discipline of economic science. It is also one reason why Marx can fittingly be called "the last of the great classical economists."[2]

In any case, Marx had the labor theory of value at hand as his fundamental building block and drew from it the logical conclusion that all value was created by the laborer. Why, then, didn't the latter keep the full value, instead of having part of it expropriated from him, and set up as an alien god, dominating his life, and subjecting him to misery and degradation?

The answer was available in Marx's theory of surplus value. After all, Marx reasoned in critical fashion, i.e., questioning fundamental assumptions, whence arises profits? The capitalist starts with capital. Combined with labor, it produces a commodity. If the capitalist gets back the capital he started with, and the laborer gets the rightful value of his work put into the commodity, how can "profit" be extracted from the productive process? Marx calls the materials and machinery supplied by the capitalist—say, cotton and yarn to be processed by Arkwright's spinning machine—"constant" capital and the worker's labor power, "variable" capital. It is only by paying the worker subsistence wages, which, for example, might equal the value of what he produces in six hours of labor, and then working him six more hours, and pocketing the value of the extra commodities thus produced (beyond the repayment of the initial capital advanced, which we will say, is equal to three hours) that the capitalist secures his profit. This, of course, as put by Marx, amounts to sheet exploitation.

Smith had said it was "to no purpose" to inquire into such deviations from the "original state of things." Marx thought otherwise, and came up with an original and even inspired handling of the matter. Presented as sober science, based, indeed, on the "Iron Law of Wages," which had been enunciated by the early classical economists themselves, Marx's formula had the additional advantage of justifying the anger occasioned by the sight of capitalists living well, even in times of commercial crises, while their "hands" starved. Workers who never read *Capital* nevertheless could now trust that there was a scientific underpinning to their feeling of being exploited.

As science, however, there were, and are, many problems with Marx's formulation. If profit only arises on "variable" capital, i.e., the use of labor power, how does one explain why manufacturers using much machinery and little labor may sometimes make larger profits than manufacturers using less machinery and much labor? Why would the manufacturer in the latter situation ever want to replace labor—the profit-creating component—with machinery? These, and other technical questions, arose to plague Marx as soon as he finished *Capital*. He was aware of the latent contradiction, and tried to wrestle with it in the two volumes that were to be published posthumously. (Profit, he declared in them, does not vary in the individual case relative to the amounts of constant and variable capital involved for the simple reason that each firm is subject to competition, which acts as a leveling force. But this, too, causes problems for Marxist economics, threatening to call into question the whole basis of the theory.)

There are further important, less technical, implications of Marx's theory of surplus value, but let us first finish with the other major theories in *Capital* before addressing ourselves to such implications. The next theory of Marx's concerns the accumulation of capital itself. Where does it initially come from? In a vivid historical treatment, Marx deals with the "primary" accumulation of capital, which he depicts not as resulting from the capitalist's hard work and savings, but from brutal confiscation, slavery, and rapine. Capital thus comes into the world, in Marx's searing prose, covered with blood from head to foot. Its accumulation "was accomplished with merciless Vandalism, and under the stimulus of passions the most infamous, the most sordid, the pettiest, the most meanly odious."[3]

Alas, one does not have to be a Marxist to agree with Marx here. The annals of history, precapitalist as well as capitalist, are not pretty. How much this "Vandalism" is built into the nature of large social systems; entwined with forms of social systems foreign to capitalism, which may persist even into postcapitalism; and embedded in human nature (whatever that is), per se, these are questions Marx dismisses with a wave of his theory of economic determinism. What is left is a graphic, and all-too-true, picture of part of the human past, toward which most of us try to numb ourselves. Marx touches a raw nerve.

In its capitalist form of accumulation, capital, Marx asserts, will tend to become more and more concentrated (there will also be a long-term decline in the rate of profit). Small firms will gobble up, or eliminate smaller ones, and become large firms; large firms will grow, by the same process, even larger. An asymptotic development toward fewer and fewer huge firms takes place, leaving fewer and fewer capitalists, with more and more of them falling into the proletariat, and the proletariat increasingly defenseless before such monstrous accumulations—the new Molochs of the market place.

Concomitantly, the law of increasing misery comes into play. Many others before Marx saw such a development taking place in the 1840s in England. Thus, Carlyle could speak of a baleful enchantment—a Midas touch—that had fallen on England, in which increasing wealth in the country at large meant increasing poverty for the mass of people.[4] Out of such observations, Marx made a "law." Subsequent events have not dealt well with Marx's "law," for in capitalist countries the lot of the majority of workers has clearly improved. Marxists have brought into play "Ptolemaic circles" to account for the new phenomena apparently contradicting the law by appealing to notions of a "labor aristocracy," based on imperialism, etc. Marx, in essence, however, had already discounted any evidence contradictory to his "law" by stating in the *Economic and Philosophic Manuscripts* that increased productivity, even if resulting in increased return to the worker, only meant a more refined form of alienation, i.e., building the capitalist juggernaut higher and more powerful only meant a more powerful oppressor of the people. Thus, in *Capital*, though Marx speaks in terms of economic laws rather than alienation, I read his analysis as still being in the service of the latter.

I have tried to highlight some of the theories in *Capital*. By concentrating on the theories, however, we miss the real meaning of the book. It is a passionate drama, an epic poem, in which we descend into capitalism's innermost circles, go through its purgatory fires, in order to emerge at the end with a glimpse of its downfall and a promise of future salvation. It is Marx's imagery, not his economic "science," which grips us; it is his judgmental wrath, not his objective analysis that fastens on *both* our hearts and minds. Listen to the Dantesque language Marx uses:

> Let us, therefore, leave this noisy region of the market, where all that goes on is done in full view of every one's eyes, where everything seems open and above board. We will follow the owner of money and the owner of labour power into the hidden foci of production, crossing the threshold of the portal above which is written, 'No admittance except on business'. Here we shall discover, not only how capital produces, but also how it is itself produced. We shall at last discover the secret of the making of surplus value.[5]

If this be economic science, Marx has made the most of it!

II

It is time to emerge from this nether world—the Hellish workshops of capitalism, where Marx pursued his particular economic theories—and look around us. The root of all evil seems to be surplus value; it embodies the exploitation of man by man. Buttressed by private property, which is the result of division of labor, the extraction of surplus value is the form in which a "have" class can grind the faces of the poor. In *Capital*, Marx felt he had demonstrated this as a matter of scientific fact (though he had twinges of uncertainty, as mentioned earlier). "Scientific socialism" appeared enshrined in the two-fold sense, now, of economic laws describing capitalism, and historical laws describing the dynamics of social change to and away from capitalism. The early, humanist Marx seemed not to be particularly relevant to the new Marxist science.

As economic science, however, the story of surplus value has been seriously challenged, as noted, by non-Marxist economists. It cannot confidently be said to be an accepted contribution to social science (though it is a fundamental contribution to Marxism as a secular religion). It is, however, suggestive, raising important questions for non-Marxists, as well as Marxists. In all societies, to rise above a subsistence level (however defined), accumulation—deferred gratification?—must occur. We can call this surplus value. Even Marx allows for what is called socially necessary labor time, i.e., to take the example I gave earlier, labor beyond the six hours required for subsistence. After all, such socially necessary labor—in capitalism taking what Marx perceived as the perverted form of "profit"—is essential if we are to reach the productive abundance required before we can enter into true communism (as distinct from "primitive communism").

The problem, then, is really not with surplus value, i.e., socially necessary labor, but with its distribution and control. How much should go immediately to the laborer, giving him more than subsistence? Are entrepreneurs necessary, and what is their proper reward? (As Joseph Schumpeter points out, Marx deals with capitalist accumulation as an impersonal, automatic process—arising after primary accumulation—and never mentions the entrepreneur as a real actor.)[6] How should the surplus value be reinvested? Who decides the proper allocations? Who, in short, controls the immediate distribution and the long-term use of socially necessary labor? What, indeed, is necessary for society, and who decides? And will this requirement disappear under communism?

Let us look first at the existing situation, as it really functions under capitalism. The fact is that Marx's assumption that surplus value is bound to be totally appropriated by the capitalist, and not shared with the worker, is based on several further assumptions. One is that all political power is necessarily controlled by the capitalist, without any significant part in that control being played by the workers, and this even in a representative democracy. Marx's political theory, inasmuch as he has one, is that the state is merely the coercive instrument of the ruling class. Bourgeois democracy is a sham.

Empirical evidence has shown otherwise. The very Parliamentary inquiries into working conditions that Marx used to damn the capitalists resulted in important ameliorations, though they were slow in coming. Ironically, it was in 1867, the very year of *Capital*, that urban workers were given the vote in Great Britain! Again slowly, but steadily, in Britain and European countries where social democracy grew, a "welfare state" came into being. By *political* means, workers could better their conditions, even if in relative terms the gap in wealth held by "haves" and "have-nots," to use such terms, did not appreciably narrow. Marx, justifiably, could claim some of the credit for pressuring the capitalist, but the consequence was a negation, so to speak, of his own prediction.

Pressure came from outside the political arena, as well as within. In parliamentary democracies, trade unions were "allowed," though grudgingly, and came to significant power in affecting the distribution of surplus value, whether in the form of wages, working conditions, or perks. Generally, the trade unions also became the vehicle for workers' participation in the political process. In Western capitalist countries, therefore, the unions did not always serve to develop Marxist class consciousness, as he had hoped, but rather integrated the workers into a modified form of the capitalist state.

It is certainly true that, under capitalism, the decisions as to the reinvestment—a major aspect of the allocation—of surplus value, i.e., capital, have been taken largely by individual entrepreneurs. Such decisions, however, are not completely independent of the democratic political process. Even in "laissez-faire" America, reinvestment is powerfully influenced by tax policy, government subventions, etc. And these are subject, in part, to a political system in which workers are also voters and, however misled from their "true" interests, play a role. In European countries, which are more oriented to social democracy, nationalized industries, Five Year Plans, and government control of the economy are signs of more direct, political, and hence partly worker, control.

The problem of control over socially necessary labor does not disappear, even where private property (at least in the form of productive forces) is officially abolished. Thus, in a so-called Communist society, "expropriation" of surplus value can occur in the name of capital accumulation; its expenditure, of course, is in the name of and for the presumed benefit of the workers (capitalists, too, claim to operate for the general good). We know, in fact, that workers in Marxist societies such as the Soviet Union, without representative government and independent trade unions, have less direct control over such decisions than in some non-Marxist societies. A non-believer, and even Marx himself, might conclude that the workers were more alienated from their labor—its product, its conditions of work, etc.—in Russia than under democratic capitalism. A Party, rather than individual entrepreneurs, makes the decisions, and not the individual workers. Thus, the "dictatorship of the proletariat" does not necessarily guarantee a less alienated form of allocation of socially necessary labor than does capitalism.

The fact is that as long as socially necessary labor exists, there will always be two parties to its existence: the laborers who create the surplus, and those who allocate and reinvest the surplus. (I have already spoken about some of the problems emanating from this fact.) Another aspect of the problem stems from Marx's conception of the worker as an abstraction, a mechanical actor in a formulaic relationship, without any particular historical character. Marx ignored the possibility that the Industrial Revolution represented the aspirations and value systems of parts of the working population as well as of the capitalists; that, rather than being imposed on the workers, the Industrial Revolution was created by them together with the capitalists. Thus, even when workers have had a clear political voice, they have not voted for the overturn of the capitalist industrial system, but for a greater share of its "surplus." (Marx, in fact, did see this, as when he bewailed trade union consciousness, but he did not let what he saw affect his theory—"what should be" triumphed over "what is.") Such behavior has been not only a result of capitalist domination over public opinion—propaganda—but because the worker has brought his own values—the desire for material improvement, for choice of occupation, for urban novelty, etc.—to the situation.

Workers are not Lockean blank tablets. As E. P. Thompson, an avowed Marxist, has brilliantly shown, the English working class was not simply created by the Industrial Revolution, but entered into its own creation, shaping itself as well as being shaped from outside.[7] Another Marxist

historian, John Foster, has shown how labor in England moved to ac-
comodation, rather than class conflict, in the Midlands in the mid-19th
century.[8] Thus, though sympathetic to Marx, Foster gives an historical
account of why Marx's predictions were in this case falsified by reality.
As Foster shows, before Marx the textile workers knew about surplus value.
One of the Oldham spinners declared to his companions, in 1835, that
the employers "seem to know no way of meeting a declining market but
that of getting more work out of you and paying you less wages . . . we
ought to ascertain the *intrinsic* value of labour; for until we have learned
that it is impossible to ascertain to what extent we are robbed of the fruit
of our labour."[9] The workers' cry lacked Marx's theoretical sophistica-
tion; it came as close to the truth, however, in its over-simplification
(i.e., not close enough), as did his elaborate explanation.

Whether in terms of economic science or historical reality, Marx's
theory of surplus value does not stand up to serious criticism. Its
philosophical assumptions, whether about political theory, worker consciousness, or capitalist behavior (as Henry Ford is reputed to have said,
raising his workers' wages to the unheard of sum of five dollars a day,
"If I don't pay them enough to buy my cars, who is going to buy them?"),
are shaky. As moral denunciation, or emotional revulsion, Marx's theory of surplus value has a power and force not to be minimized. As a
piece of economic science, it has little value, other than as pointing to
a problem.

Standing as it does at the heart of *Capital*, Marx' theory of surplus
value allows us to probe the real meaning of that great work. *Capital*,
first of all, offers us a magnificent historical drama: the story of how
capitalists exploited the workers in 19th-century England. It employs a
masterly exposition of classical economic theory, with original addi-
tions, which it then applies to the epic conflict of the classes. It animates the whole with passionate indignation and prophetic zeal. Thus,
though it does employ social analysis, *Capital* is fundamentally a chosen instrument—the Worker's Bible, as Engels had said—in Marx's eschatological mission to spark a revolution.

III

Marx's real insight was embodied in the materialist, or economic, interpretation of history, spelled out in the early works such as *The German*

Ideology. It is the mainspring of his greatness. Though foreshadowed by James Harrington, Adam Smith, and others—Marx himself acknowledges Guizot and Thierry—its perception was only made feasible by the events of the Industrial Revolution; still, it was Marx who most deeply and importantly realized that the developing productive forces of a society create new social relations. Thus, he bound economics to sociology. In place of "political economy" he offers an economically-based sociology.

In turn, Marx's "economic conditions of production" are based on tools. Benjamin Franklin had called man "the tool-making animal," and Marx, quoting him, accepted this definition of man's nature. Marx then went on to emphasize the history of technology (and, inferentially, the history of science). Where the French *Encyclopédie* gave a static description of the existing state of the arts and sciences—a taxonomy, so to speak—Marx offered an evolutionary perspective—his true claim to be in the Darwinian mode. What is more, he understood that technology does not develop in a vacuum, but is a result of social processes; and affects society in turn, a lesson still apparently in need of absorption today.

The result is an enormously powerful vision of how social analysis should take place. Marx linked the surging mechanization of his time, which has swelled to such heights in ours, to the increasing dominance of economic transactions, and placed them both in the service of social forces. History of technology, economics, and sociology; these subjects are made whole, as they should be; no wonder so many modern scholars have been attracted to the Marxist synthesis.

The problems arise when this has been said. Marx, taken as the letter of his "law," is quite different from Marx in the spirit. He himself linked his great revolutionary insight to an equally great incubus: the conviction that he could now *predict*, more or less precisely, what future social relations would have to be, i.e., communism. What was analysis turns into eschatology. What were empirically based observations in the 1840s slide into dogmatic assertions by Marx and his followers after the 1850s and 1860s, in the face of new developments and later in the face of new evidence in subsequent periods.

On one side, for example, the "production" of the proletariat, or factory workers, by the Industrial Revolution gives way in the 20th century to other developments: service workers, computer freaks, etc. What does it mean to talk in Marxist terms of "workers of the world unite" when for example, students in France in the 1980s outnumber the workers of General Motors, the largest capitalist-industrial enterprise in the world? (Incidentally, the hammer and sickle is a good symbolic representation of the outmoded conception of workers' work held by the Communists; in the 20th century, work is more aptly symbolized by power tools, etc.) We have seen the problems involved with the workers of Marx's own time, who did not even then believe correctly as to class consciousness. Workers today, instead of being more and more concentrated and ground down, are more and more differentiated and "embourgeoised."

On another side, though technology is undoubtedly tied to the economic and social forces of a society, it cannot be treated simply as a mere dependent variable. It has a logic partly of its own, a semi-autonomous, or "internal" aspect. And it responds to other shaping influences than merely the economic, such as military and political events. (The nuclear bomb is a prime example.) In his best moments, Marx knew this to be so. As a Marxist, he chose to ignore the complexities of actual social analysis, the way in which technological, economic, political, social, and intellectual factors *all* interact, in changing and variable fashion. The result is reductionism and dogma. The great insight is betrayed.

Yet the original discernment remains. It leads to another perception: that economics is connected not only to tools and society, but to politics. Again, this is hardly a novel idea. But Marx gives it a depth and resonance that it had not previously had. "The Eighteenth Brumaire" and "The Class Struggles in France" are brilliant exemplifications. Once more, however, Marx tends to "reduce" the phenomenon. I have called him before a *terrible simplificateur:* politics becomes merely a consequence of the economic conditions of production. Marx himself fluctuated, as later Marxists do, between speaking of determinism (strict and loose), influence, correspondence, and so forth. What he did not allow for was that political action, unrooted in the economic conditions, an act of *will,* such as Lenin's Bolshevik seizure of power, could change the course of history. Once in place, Bolshevism then had to *produce* the economic conditions that were supposed to have produced it as a political consequence. Marx's affinity for inversion, it would seem, had taken an unintended turn.

Marx's *camera obscura* had revealed to him that consciousness was connected to material conditions, that ideas were not independent of the circumstances in which they were formed. Others had spoken of a "climate of opinions"; Marx inquired into class consciousness and "ruling ideas." He founded what is today called the "sociology of knowledge." Again, as an analytic tool, Marx's conception is an important one. However, as with all of his ideas, it can be reduced to a dogma, a tool not for analysis but for the inculcation of revolutionary sentiment. We have already noted the problems with actual worker class consciousness and the way in which, as the "worker" changes, other problems arise. Class consciousness, therefore, is not a final statement, but must be the beginning of a truly empirical inquiry.

Nevertheless, whatever the problems, of reductionism, of application, etc., the value of Marx's cognitive contributions cannot be denied and ought not to be downplayed. I am arguing, however, that economic interpretation of history is not the same as an economic theory. It need not entail "laws," as the latter presumes to do. As an economist, Marx suffered from the very limits built into the classical theory by his predecessors; he never did break the "fetters" of the labor theory of value, the iron law of wages, etc. He was bound by the circumstances of his times and its ideas.

Only in his sociological vision did he transcend these limitations. The result is an analytic perspective of enduring value. Parts of Marxism, therefore, are valid contributions to social science, promising efforts at analysis rather than eschatology. These parts, however, do not add up to Marxism, the secular religion. Having indeed demystified aspects of capitalism, Marx, alas, ended by setting up his own mystification.

IX

The Importance of Being Karl Marx

In the light of all I have been saying, does it really matter who Karl Marx was? Does it matter that he was a person such as I have depicted him, and lived the life I have described, and not some other? Do we not have his doctrines, independent of his actual existence, which speak for themselves? Even if someone else had written them, would not their effect on us be the same?

Common sense would seem to nod its head in the affirmative. Yet, before we all find ourselves like those mandarin dolls, wagging our chins up and down, I suggest we examine this set of questions more closely. I think we will find a series of complicated and interrelated issues wrapped up in the seemingly simple set. The importance of being Karl Marx, and not, say, some other Marx (one of my waggish friends has suggested as a title for this book "The Grouchy Marx") or, indeed, some other named person entirely, is worth further examination. It can best be approached, however, by indirection.

I began this book by stating that Marx was the founder of a great, secular religion. I compared him to Jesus, Buddha, and Muhammad. Let us pursue the comparison further, for our present purposes. I should like to draw an analogy especially with Jesus in order to raise the necessary questions about the meaning of ideas and doctrines. Does it matter who Jesus was? That he lived the life we are told he did? I shall ask you to make a number of thought-experiments, in spite of their seeming, initially, to be blasphemous.

First, imagine that we had only one surviving account, St. Matthew's, for example, would this affect our view of Christianity? Next, imagine that we have all the existing accounts, but that suddenly, another authenticated document appeared, which gave new details of Jesus' life and behavior, somewhat at variance with the present received accounts. Say, that, in fact, it showed beyond possible doubt that Jesus was actually a charlatan, a person like Jim Jones of the People's Temple, misleading and traducing his followers. That he had taken bribes from the money lenders on the side and had actually had an affair with Mary Magdalene.

Remember, these are thought-experiments. Would they change our view of Christian doctrine? After all, the existing doctrines might be exactly the same, the words in the New Testament as we have always had them. I believe that most Christians would experience a tremendous shock at such revelations. While some Christians would undoubtedly and undoubtingly close their eyes to the new evidence and continue to believe—"believe because it is absurd," said St. Thomas Aquinas—many others would lose "faith."

In the case of Christianity, of course, a special factor is involved. Part of the doctrine, in fact, is to follow the example of Jesus. The imitation of Christ is central to the religion itself. We are exhorted to follow him, abandoning our fathers and mothers in the process, both doctrinally and existentially. If his life turned out to be a mockery of his doctrines, an obvious problem would be created.

In historical fact, we know almost nothing of Jesus, the person. Many have gone in search of him, but he is lost in the mists of time and tradition. One who made an earnest and interesting effort is Albert Schweitzer, with his *The Psychiatric Study of Jesus.*[1] Dr. Schweitzer's book reads like a case study. Various scholars, working from the existing accounts "as gospel," have portrayed Jesus as a disturbed young man, suffering from visions, hallucinations, and a split personality: a classic schizoid case. Schweitzer discusses these accounts, but at the end rescues Jesus from the asylum by declaring that the young man's behavior was completely "normal" in 33 A.D., in terms of his culture. What would be bizarre in 20th-century America was commonplace in Israel two thousand years ago, and Christ's mission could only be undertaken and carried out in the prevailing modes. Nevertheless, our fanciful thought-experiments and Schweitzer's examination do suggest that it would matter who the real Jesus was.

II

Our analogy to Jesus takes us only a little way. An air of unreality hangs about it, for we know so little about the actual man. Perhaps a more contemporary example can sharpen the issue, alerted as we are now to some of the possible speculations. Indeed, it was in relation to Henry David Thoreau that I first found myself thinking seriously and sustainedly about the problem. A new book, *Young Man Thoreau* (1975), by Richard Lebeaux, suggested that a close look at the hero's life revealed a disparity between the exhortations to independence and "life in the woods" of *Walden* and the actual experiences and behavior of the author.[2] A subsequent faculty seminar, given by one of my colleagues at the Massachusetts Institute of Technology, dissolved into a contentious discussion as to whether the new evidence made, or should make, any difference in our reception of the book's ideas.

Now Thoreau is a particularly apt comparison to Marx. As it happens, he was a direct contemporary, born in 1817, a year earlier than the father of scientific socialism. The first chapter of *Walden* is on "Economy." Ostensibly, it is on the "economy" of Thoreau's household arrangements at the pond—the food, clothing, and shelter encapsulated in the original Greek meaning of the word "economy"—and on living "economically," i.e., sparsely. In fact, a closer look reveals that *Walden*, begun in 1844 (though published in 1854), is at least as much a critique of commercial civilization, of the industrializing society of mid-19th-century America, as it is an encomium of life in the woods.

Like his German counterpart, Thoreau laments the decay of man in a mercantile society, where "the laboring man has not leisure for a true integrity day by day; he cannot afford to sustain the manliest relations to man; his labor would be depreciated in the market." So, too, the note of alienation and dehumanization is sounded: the laborer "has no time to be anything but a machine," for "men have become the tool of their tools." As for the basic principle of modern capitalist society, division of labor, Thoreau also disdains it, as when he rhetorically asks, "Where is this division of labor to end? and what object does it finally serve?"[3]

Thus, the two men, Thoreau and Marx, deal with the same subject, i.e., the effect of the industrial revolution on man, and share the same critical attitude toward it. Their solutions, however, differ profoundly. Marx, as we have seen, recoiled in horror from the accusation of egotism; Thoreau embraces it wholeheartedly, declaring that the correct life consists of securing one's own integrity rather than reforming society. On his very first page, treating of "Economy," Thoreau announces, "In most books, the I, or first person is omitted; in this it will be retained; that, in respect to egotism, is the main difference." His justification is that "I should not talk so much about myself if there were anybody else whom I knew as well." As a result, where Marx turned primarily to Hegelian dialectics and economic theories, Thoreau claimed to be turning to his own "economic" experiences as the source of solutions to his society's industrial woes.

As part of his "egotism," Thoreau also, unlike Marx, rejects the accumulated "progress" of the past. He does this, first, in relation to the preceding generation: "I have lived some thirty years on this planet, and I have yet to hear the first syllable of valuable or even earnest advice from my seniors." Next, he extends his disdain to historical evolution, which he sees, not as a progressive dialectic à la Hegel, but as a fall from pristine goodness. "I think the fall from the farmer to the operative [i.e., the shift from agriculture to the factory] as great and memorable as that from the man to the farmer." In short, for our purpose here is not to explore the full dimensions of Thoreau's thought, his solution, unlike Marx's, is not to move toward a communist society, built on the accumulated, historical capital of the preceding generations, but to return to the primitive, self-sufficient state of the solitary individual.*

---

* I need to make it very clear that I am dealing here not with Thoreau in the round, but mainly as a critic of modern society who, implicitly when not explicitly, is recommending another way of life. From another perspective, one could focus (as most literary scholars have done) on Thoreau as an artist, a writer, who comes to be one by a self-transformation whose vehicle is itself his writing. He goes to Walden Pond to make a new man of himself, by producing *Walden*. In such a view, his spiritual experience is real. Inasmuch as we participate in it, it is also real for us.

Such an interpretation places its weight on Thoreau's inner experience, its validity for him. It accords with his "egotism" and his insistence that his mode of living is for himself alone. It may also correspond to our personal need. I believe it naïve, however, to think that this is all that Thoreau intended. In as much as there is an external, public side to Thoreau's experience—his self-transformation is to serve as an inspiration or model for ours and his society's—then for reasons given in my text there is also an inauthentic quality to it in precisely the terms I spell out. The problem I am addressing is not his spiritual

It is very American: Adam in the new world paradise; the frontiers-man in the wilderness. In going to Walden Pond, the young Thoreau claims to have found his true and proper identity. It is a personal solution, which also claims to be a solution to the social problem of the 1840s. In spite of disclaimers to the contrary, *de rigueur* for his independent, individualist philosophy—"I would not have any one adopt *my* mode of living on any account; for, beside that before he has fairly learned it I may have found out another for myself, I desire that there may be as many different persons in the world as possible"—it is evident that Thoreau is presenting his life experiences to us as a model of how a man should live (it is noteworthy that there is hardly a word about women).

Lebeaux, in the conclusion of *Young Man Thoreau*, puts it well when he says, "It is this persona, this 'presence'—rather than the historical Thoreau—which has captured the imagination of so many Americans. In writing *Walden*, Thoreau created a myth of personality and experience which helped to sustain him, and which has given inspiration and hope to others."[4] Working out his own personal transformation, I would add, or at least claiming to do so, the author of *Walden* invites us to believe that we, too, can effect a self-transformation; and, in so doing, transcend our increasingly commercial, industrial culture. By writing of his purported experience, Thoreau creates an "idea," which then has the power to lead other men into similar experiences, or at least the achieving of a similar personal identity.

The fallout for society is less clear. Unlike Marx, Thoreau offers little in the way of a social science. He does offer, however, a *praxis* of sorts: live as he does, independent of other men, free from the division of labor and the ambitions of increased affluence. (In another part of his work, he also recommends the "action" of civil disobedience, which does, and did, have direct social and reforming consequences; but it, too, is in the service of his independent mode of life.)

This is the Thoreau most of us know (if we know him at all). What if it turns out that the real, historical Thoreau is different from his persona? Should this disclosure in any way affect our judgment of his philosophy and his recommendations about life? Does it make us any less

---

rebirth, or self-therapy by means of what one scholar, Leo Marx, calls his "extravagant idealization of himself"—nor the quality of the literary works that emerge from this regeneration—but the validity of his experience as a social cure.

likely to concur with his ideas, and make them our own? Should it? These questions take on concrete life in the light of Lebeaux's book, which is the starting point for my reflections.

According to Lebeaux, young Thoreau was a deeply conflicted individual: with strong feelings about his "failed" father, ambivalent about his dependency feelings toward his mother, tormented by competitive feelings towards his brother, etc. The interpretation is Eriksonian, filled with references to the life cycle, identity crisis, and the other terms made ubiquitous by the author of *Young Man Luther*. I am not concerned here, however, with this facet of the book, but rather with its evidence that, for whatever reasons, Thoreau's account is at variance with his own experiences. He, who "brag[ged]," "as lustily as chanticleer in the morning . . . if only to wake my neighbors up," about his vaunted independence and self-sufficiency, was, in fact, only bragging.[5]

One scholar, Channing, cited by Lebeaux tells us that "some have fancied because he moved to Walden he left his family. He bivouacked there, and really lived at home, where he went every day." Another, Harding, is quoted by Lebeaux:

> Thoreau visited the village, or was visited at Walden, almost every day. Such people as Emerson, the Alcotts, and the children of Concord visited often. Some Concordians, says Harding, "claimed that 'he would have starved, if it had not been that his sisters and mother cooked up pies and doughnuts and sent them to him in a basket.' . . . The Emersons, too, frequently invited him to dinner, as did the Alcotts and the Hosmers. They had all done so before he went to Walden Pond and continued the custom after he left. Rumor had it that every time Mrs. Emerson rang her dinner bell, Thoreau came bounding through the woods and over the fences to be the first in line at the Emerson dinner table."[6]

Of all this, Thoreau admits nothing in *Walden*. He thus misleads us, even if only by omission.

With our eye now altered, we can ourselves return to the book, able to see discrepancies. We can remember that Thoreau himself acknowledges that his tools are borrowed, i.e., he is dependent on his neighbors ("It is difficult to begin without borrowing," he confesses.).[7] If we know anything outside *Walden* about Thoreau's life, we can reread his statement about living thirty years without hearing anything valuable from his seniors—and recall that Thoreau himself acknowledged that his six-week stay with Orestes Brownson in Canton, Massachusetts in 1836 affected him profoundly, declaring the period "a new era in my life";[8] and even more to the point is his relation to Ralph Waldo Emerson, fourteen years his senior, i.e., of another generation, who, starting in 1837–38 became his revered teacher and second-father, and who, in fact, owned the fourteen acres of woodland bordering Walden Pond, where, starting in 1845, Thoreau took up his immortal "independent" existence.

So what? the reader may say to this and other such evidence. Thoreau's message has a validity independent (if I may pun) of whether or not he actually lived the independent life about which he bragged. And so, up to a point, I am inclined to agree. I would argue further, however, that it does matter, in at least one particular and important way. If Thoreau's own "experience" was not as he reported, then it cannot serve as evidence for the liveability of his ideas. The ideas may still be "right," but we have no evidential grounds on which to come to that conclusion.

Rather, we may have grounds to believe that we are in the presence of a fantasy, with all the pro and con that may entail. The historical Thoreau, not the chanticleer of *Walden*, actually speaks to us about an adolescent, somewhat delayed, who has no fixed job as understood by ordinary men; no wife, or loved one, or sexual relations of any kind; and no dependents, i.e., children, except for himself; in short, not about a mature adult. *Walden* is, therefore, profoundly misleading as an exemplar of how a real, complete life should be lived.

Let me hasten to add, it is brilliant, powerful, and well worth reading. So is *Robinson Crusoe* (of which it is a modern version). As long as we recognize that it is largely a fantasy and can distinguish it from reality (which, of course, it can nevertheless illuminate), we gain from reading it. It is when we allow it to inspire us as in the 1960s, to become a hippie, to "drop out" of society, that it may (and I emphasize may) be misleading us in a direction and to an identity which we have followed under the false belief that it had already been tested and found valid.

Thoreau, though criticizing industrial society, is speaking to the individual and offering an individual fantasy. Only indirectly, and very indirectly, is he advocating a vision of a new society (actually, a return to an old one), or offering us a social theory by which to reshape ourselves and society. As with Jesus, and our imitation of his life, the inauthenticity of Thoreau's experience would seem to be cause for a reexamination of our commitment to his ideas. If *he* could not authentically live his ideas, why should we assume we can; or that the ideas can, in fact, be so lived at all? It *is* important, consequently, who Thoreau was. Especially telling in this regard is that Thoreau had said that he knew himself best, thus validating his account. In fact, he portrayed not his true self, but a fiction. Not knowing even himself well, could he really presume to know authentically about us, the rest of human kind? Or the kind of society in which we should live the good life, on real terms?

III

With Marx, we have a thinker who goes well beyond Thoreau's efforts, and offers us, overtly, a social theory, a social science, and a vision of the good society. How, in the light of what we have said about Jesus and Thoreau, do we now regard the question of "The Importance of Being Karl Marx"? To repeat: Does it matter what sort of person the author of the *Communist Manifesto* and *Capital* really was?

On reflection, the analogy of Marx to such figures as Jesus and Thoreau may not be entirely appropriate. In their case, imitation of the life— and thus the life itself—is intrinsic to the doctrine. Marx never proposed himself as a model for his followers, or asked them to follow him in this regard. Whether he was a scoundrel or a saint, he would have argued, could in no way affect the validity of his ideas and theories.

His followers seemed to think otherwise. In spite of Marx's attitude toward the role of personalities in history, they have come close to deifying him. The official reminiscences, while allowing for a few human blemishes, paint a picture of a good-natured, good-humored giant, a doting son, husband, and father, whose whole life is unegotistically and selflessly devoted to the cause of revolution and the masses. His picture (along with Engels), blown up, smiles benignly and wisely down on Red Square and other communist public and private spaces in god-like fashion.

Revolutions, like religions, it seems, need persons to imitate. In the early days of the French Revolution, Robespierre was the figure of Virtue incarnate; then, in the failing days of the Revolution under the Directory, it was Babeuf. His personal character, and the story of his conspiracy and martyrdom, took on legendary features, and became an inspiration for the revolutionary underground of the early 19th century.

Blanqui, his successor, was in the same mold. It was his example rather than his doctrines that attracted youthful followers. As one biographer, Patrick Hutton, puts it, "Blanqui was for his disciples more than a living archive of past revolutionary glories. He was a model of revolutionary asceticism. His followers stood in awe of the patience with which he endured imprisonment for most of his adult life. Those who shared his confinement pointedly comment upon the quasimonastic regimen of work, conversation, and exercise from which he never permitted himself the slightest departure." As Hutton concludes, "His appeal to the youth movement which assumed his name in the latter half of the nineteenth century was in the authenticity of a way of life grounded in moral passion."[9]

Marx never consciously wished for such identification. Nevertheless, his apparent selfless dedication, his sacrifice of comfort and family to the revolutionary cause—the revolutionary ascetic qualities I mentioned earlier—did make him an example to others. Many followers, at least, presumed that the purity of the revolution was somehow connected to the purity of its doctrinal founder. Thus, for years, the Soviet Union suppressed the evidence in its archives as to Marx's adultery with Lenchen and the illegitimate child produced therefrom, just as Marx had repressed it during his life. Communists today either try to turn their heads or pooh-pooh this matter as a meaningless piece of scandal, meant to discredit Marx and Communism.

Such reaction points to the fact that many people do think it matters. The message, for them, is affected by the nature of the messenger. Is this mere human frailty, which we should disregard, or an intuition to be heeded? Let us press on with our inquiry.

Is it not true that in various areas of human endeavor, such as the natural sciences, the validity of a theory is totally independent of its discover's personal attributes? To take one example: is the validity of Einstein's theory of relativity affected one way or another by the fact that he more or less abandoned the children of his first marriage when they were ten and four years old (which he did), or that he was a warm, kind, loving friend to his co-workers and mankind (which he was)?[10] The answer is clearly "no." Theories in natural science are verified, or at least not falsified, on other grounds than the scientist's personal life.

We may be interested in the scientist's biography for other reasons. We may be vicariously curious about how he came to be a scientist, what the life of a scientist is really like, and how his creativity came to be developed. Some of us might even believe, in principle, that there might be some connection between his personality and his theories, but have no hope of tracing it out. I confess this was my position, until I heard my friend, Gerald Holton, lead a two-day seminar in Stockbridge, Massachusetts, at the suggestion of Erik Erikson, on Albert Einstein and his work. To my amazement, Holton was able to relate traits of Einstein's personality to statements and formulae in the 1905 papers on relativity in a meaningful way. It was almost as if one could see Einstein's characterological thumbprints in the paper itself!

Even in the most recondite papers on physics, then, personality, on this account, does seem to matter, in the limited sense of leaving some discernible trace. I myself am convinced of this fact in the less mathematical field of 19th-century biology, where the imprint of Darwin's personality can be found in many places in the theory of evolution by natural selection. Yet even here, the validation of the theory, once created or discovered, stands apart from the life of its progenitor.

Is this the case with Marx and his work? Or is he closer to Jesus and Thoreau, after all? Let us see. Natural science, we are told, is cumulative. As Newton remarked, he stood on the shoulders of giants; it is implied that if he hadn't sighted his theories of optics and gravitation, someone else would have. Indeed, the differential calculus was invented simultaneously by Newton and Leibnitz. Even Darwin found his "double" in Alfred Russel Wallace, who in 1858 independently promulgated the theory of evolution by natural selection. Was Marx, too, we must ask, merely the product of his "climate of opinion," or the state of science at his time, and, if he had not come along, replaceable by someone else? In short, the implication of all that we have said about natural science is that personality doesn't matter very much.

The fact is we are now in deep waters. These are highly involved and difficult questions in the philosophy of science. Though the validity of the differential calculus stands apart from its discoverer, those in the know say that the "style" of the two men, Newton and Leibnitz, was very different and had powerful effects on their relative followers and thus the course of mathematics in England and Germany. Though the theory of evolution by natural selection stands or falls on "non-personal" evidence, it mattered greatly that it was Charles Darwin, rather than Wallace, who publicly fathered the theory. Wallace, a relatively unknown amateur would have had his paper buried in some obscure journal; Darwin was a part of the Establishment, to whom attention had to be paid. The whole attendant paraphernalia of social Darwinism (Wallace had socialist tendencies, and was anti-imperialist), eugenics, implications for religion, etc., would have differed.

Nevertheless, though the outriders, so to speak, of theories in natural science may differ, the strong implication is that personality is only accountable for the errors, not the verifiable findings of the scientist. Once the theory is promulgated and propagated, its value is totally independent of the theorist himself. It could be Joe Doaks, instead of Newton or Einstein, who stands as the scientist in back of gravitation or relativity. The phenomenon exists on its own merits, and the personality doesn't affect the validity of the theory developed to account for it.

Science is "impersonal," in these terms. Oddly enough, the endeavor perceived as most opposite to natural science is also read in the same manner. Literature and art are the most personal of all products, but the artist's personality is generally judged to have little to do with the value of his creation. Van Gogh may have cut off his ear to send to a girl-friend and gone insane at the end of his life, but our judgment of the aesthetic worth of his pictures remains, or ought to remain, unaffected by such biographical detail. Do we really care, as we read Byron's poems, that he may have had an incestuous affair with his halfsister?

Matters can, of course, get political. During World War I, Beethoven and Brahms, as German musicians, were banned from concert halls in the United States. Today, Wagner cannot be performed in Israel. (We might recall that, in science, relativity theory was denounced in Nazi Germany because Einstein was a Jew, with perhaps more serious consequences for the German nation than Israel's abstinence from Wagner visited on itself.) Ezra Pound's poetry was attacked because of his association with Fascist Italy. Yet, though occasionally the effort is made to condemn the music or the poetry because of its creator—guilt by association—most of us recognize the difference between an aesthetic and a political judgment. St. Thomas Aquinas's medieval distinction between acts of "doing" and "being"—i.e., deeds, which can be moral or immoral; and products, which are either good or bad aesthetically—still largely holds today (separate from this issue is the moral effect of a work of art, e.g. a drama leading to lascivious or violent behavior).

IV

Where in all this discussion do we place Karl Marx? He was neither simply a natural scientist nor an artist. Marx thought of himself as a social scientist (although what this meant for him, especially as his thought developed in his later works, was a kind of natural scientist whose area of inquiry was human affairs). His language in the Preface of 1867 to the first German edition of *Capital* testifies to his desired identity: "Intrinsically, it is not a question of the higher or lower degree of development of the social antagonisms that result from the natural laws of capitalist production. It is a question of these laws themselves, of these tendencies working with iron necessity towards inevitable results."[11] In this same spirit, he compared himself to Darwin, claiming to do for social history what the latter had done for natural history.

I cannot follow Marx in this assertion. The problem is that the social sciences are *sui generis*, partaking on one side of the humanities and on the other of the sciences. The claim to "science," in the sense of the natural sciences, with their generalizations, law-like statements, and theories open to experimental testing, is suspect. The attempt, as in physics, to simplify and to subsume more and more partial theories under a more general one runs counter to the reality of the social or human sciences, where ambiguities mount, historical reruns are impossible, the subject matter—man—is part of the solution, and a key problem is how to deal with "what should be" as well as "what is."

This is not the place finally to decide the nature of the social sciences. For our purposes, I need only hint, as I have, at the way it differs from both the natural sciences and the arts. The fact is that Marx, on one side, is offering us a vision of the way the world ought to be—it is almost a literary vision—at the same time as he declares its realization to be a matter of scientific certainty, i.e., social science. Are the vision and the certainty separable from his personality as, it may be argued, Van Gogh's visionary paintings (or Thoreau's fantasy?) and Einstein's theory of relativity are from theirs?

If Marx were like Einstein, a scientist in a cumulative tradition, we could argue that "scientific socialism" was a necessary discovery, Marx or no Marx. Someone else would have come up with the same theories. After all, similar theories were, indeed, in the air. A glance back at the earlier chapters of this book shows how Marx borrowed from Hegel and Feuerbach, Smith and the other classical economists, and a whole host of utopian and other socialists. My point is joined exactly here: although the climate of opinion made possible Marx's synthesis, that synthesis was uniquely his. He alone, the particular person, Karl Marx, made possible the fusion we know as Marxism. His very nastiness and combativeness, for example, I am asserting, was necessary to his personal vision, to Marxism.

After Marxism exists, we can say that someone else could have developed it. Marxist theory would exist, just as the theory of gravitation, or relativity, or evolution by natural selection, independent of its particular progenitor. I do not believe this. No one but Marx could have developed Marxism as we know it. In saying this, I am also implicitly saying that Marx's theories are not "scientific," in the natural science sense.

What about his theories as social science? After all, unlike a Thoreau, Marx does claim to offer us such a science (which we can free from his confusion as to its being equivalent to a natural science). Here we are on different ground. For example, how should we evaluate, or validate, Marx's theory that "history is the history of class struggle"? It seems, as presented in Marx's assertive prose, a persuasive statement, a piece of respectable social science.

In fact, it is historically suspect, to say the least. Class is a 19th-century term, referring to economic divisions created by the Industrial Revolution. It replaces earlier usage of orders, estates, ranks, and so forth (Adam Smith habitually spoke of ranks). It is a useful, nay, essential, term in analyzing social stratification in modern society, i.e., in industrial society. It is anachronistic, however, to impose it on earlier and other forms of society, where stratification on other than economic grounds—religious, political, ethnic, etc.—is more important.[12] It does not particularly help to explain the struggle of Guelphs and Ghibelines in Dante's Florence, the crusading wars of medieval Christians and Muslims, etc.

Marx's purpose is obviously polemical. The social scientific validity of his "theory" of class struggle is not his major concern. The theory itself is a reflection of Marx's perception of the world and is rooted in his own instinctual needs—we cannot help remembering his obsession with "endless strife" in his early poetry, his emphasis on struggle and strength, and his own combative nature—and his effort to forge an integrated self, which he tried to realize in his struggle for a coherent sense of the world. As a cognitive matter, "class struggle" is less an acute historical generalization than a perceptive awareness of a contemporary situation, shared by many of his contemporaries—one thinks of Disraeli's "two nations" among countless other such references—but made into a "terrible simplification" (to use Jacob Burckhardt's evocative phrase) by Marx, for personal and political reasons. It also becomes prescriptive: strength and struggle is the right way. As such it takes on the quality of self-fulfilling prophecy: although class struggle is not an accurate generalization from the past, it may inspire the proletariat to give life to it as a generalization in the future.

With all this said, the critical reader may still withhold consent from my argument. "You are committing the etiological fallacy," he may point out, "of confusing the origin of Marx's theory of the class struggle in his personal nature with the question of its validity." Then, generously, the reader may add, "Your appeal to the historical evidence persuades me that the class struggle theory is poor social science—shallow and limited—but your relating it to Marx's personality is immaterial and unnecessary."

At this point, I ought to rest content. But I am not. Somewhere in these arguments, the intuition of the average person that Marx's character and behavior, as with Jesus' and Thoreau's, does matter is being lost sight of. The reason, I believe, still lies in the confusion between social science and natural science. The former, while it, too, tries to be as objective as possible (an effort, incidentally, which I strongly favor), is necessarily subjective. It is so, not only in the sense that human beings are involved in formulating the theories, but in the more important sense that they are formulating them for other humans to live by.

Philosophy, Nietzsche remarked, is the confession of the philosopher.[13] So, I would assert, is social science. However disguised, it tells us about "what should be" as well as "what is." In Marx, this is especially evident. His social "philosophy," although he repudiates the term, is inextricably mixed with his social "science." His disclaimers aside, he is prescribing the way all men should live, just as much as, indeed even more so than, was Thoreau. And the way they should live, for example, locked in class struggle, mirrors Marx's own personal needs. He is constructing a new world to replace the one surrounding and conditioning him, one which would be deeply satisfying for a world of Marxes.

At this point, the question becomes one of psychology as much as of sociology. Is Marx's view of human nature sufficiently realistic? Sigmund Freud, for example, thought not. Abstaining from judgment on the details of Marx's investigations into the economic structure of society, Freud did lament the lapse of Marxism into dogma, and, more importantly, questioned its view that "economic motives are the only ones that determine the behaviour of human beings in society." Marxism, Freud added, in abolishing others' illusions, seemed to have developed its own illusion: that Marxism would "in the course of a few generations so alter human nature that people will live together almost without friction in the new order of society, and that they will undertake the duties of work without any compulsions" seemed improbable to Freud.[14]

We do not have to be Freudians to raise the question as to what role aggression, for example, plays in human affairs. Did Marx believe his own aggressive and ambitious "feelings"—we remember his poem by that name—came only from the economic conditions of society? His own father Heinrich's response, subjective as it was, to what he called an *"embittered"* letter from his son must give us pause:

> Frankly speaking, my dear Karl, I do not like this modern word, which all weaklings use to cloak their feelings when they quarrel with the world because they do not possess, without labour or trouble, well-furnished palaces with vast sums of money and elegant carriages. This embitterment disgusts me and you are the last person from whom I would expect it. What grounds can you have for it? Has not everything smiled on you ever since your cradle? Has not nature endowed you with magnificent talents? Have not your parents lavished affection on you? Have you ever up to now been unable to satisfy your reasonable wishes? And have you not carried away in the most incomprehensible fashion the heart of a girl whom thousands envy you? Yet the first untoward event, the first disappointed wish, evokes embitterment! Is that strength? Is that a manly character?** [15]

Marx, in youth and adulthood, is necessarily the first source of his own understanding of human nature and its possibilities. What *was* his own nature? I have tried to delineate its features as manifested in his life and work. What awareness did he have of his own nature? He was not given to introspection. Did he have at hand a satisfactory psychological science, an "objective," cognitive account of man's mental and emotional processes? It appears not. Did history supply him with an "experimental laboratory," revealing the operations of human nature in a manner that would allow him confidentally to generalize about the future? The historical record concerning human nature appears to testify against Marx's hopes. It is at this point, it would appear, that Marx's

** I have used here the translation as given in Marx and Engels's *Collected Works*, which has now become the standard edition in English. The word translated there as "embitterment" is *Zerrissenheit*. Douglas Scott, who has done an excellent translation of Werner Blumenberg's book on Marx, prefers the English word "confused" rather than "embittered". *Zerrissenheit* means literally, "torn condition" and is a Romantic term for "melancholy" or "unhealthy state of mind."

own nature—his own psychological dynamics and aspirations—combines with the "what should be–what is" problem in social science: man, as a self-creating, independent creature, Marx seems to be saying, could, by will, impose himself on what is, in spite of the fact that "what is" has its own "necessary" laws.

There is an alternative argument that Marx (or Marxists) could employ. "All right," he could say, "I'm sometimes embittered, aggressive, back-biting, hypocritical, prejudiced—whatever you want to call me— in short, not the sort of person I'd ideally like to be. But that has nothing to do with my projection of how people will be under communism. My undesirable character traits are a result of the conditions and institutions that have shaped me. A different society, and I and everyone else would be entirely different."*** The response must be, "Of course you would be different, but different doesn't mean perfect; you'd have new human "flaws," and these would have untidy consequences for the society as well."

In *The German Ideology*, Marx had declared, "In revolutionary activity, change of self coincides with change of circumstances."[17] He believed that communism meant not only a just society, but a new, redeemed man. Unlike the "driven" Marxes of this world, harmonious and loving humans would be the sole inhabitants of the world to come. It is this faith of Marx's which leads me to claim that the eschatological vision overwhelms his efforts at social science—and, within Marxism, distorts and vitiates them. It turns human nature into divine nature.

Marx's hopes and aims were natural and constructive. Dreams and fantasies can be constructive and creative ways of approaching reality, if understood as ways *into* reality rather than as mere substitutions *for* reality. It is psychologically healthy to try to change the world to fit our particular nature, as well as to change ourselves to fit the existing world more satisfactorily. It is understanding of this fact, not condemnation,

***Rousseau, Godwin, and others before Marx had made the argument in equally passionate terms. Evil, for example, Rousseau contended, is not in human nature, but in society only. We are corrupted by wicked, artificial institutions. It is against this view that Malthus, in turn, wrote his *Population*. As he said, "The great error [of Rousseau and Godwin] . . . is the attributing of almost all the vices and misery that are seen in civil society to human institutions."[16] Malthus's "nature" was not just human nature, though rooted in its propensities to consume and procreate, but certain "givens," mathematical limits to human existence. Marx, as we can see, is resuming the Rousseau-Godwin position, and attacking not only Malthus's economics but implicitly his general ideas as well.

that needs to be brought to bear on Marx and Marxism. We should try to extract particular and useful pieces of "social science" from Marx's doctrines, yet realizing that this is to be distinguished from embracing his completed system.

In this light, it *does* matter, and powerfully so, who Marx actually was; a different Marx, and we would have a different utopian view of the future. Without his own struggle over the accusation of egotism, there would be a different quality to his views on money, competition, and alienation. Greater self-awareness and introspection on Marx's part would have meant a different sense of human nature and its needs in others—and thus of the sort of society *they* would construct and that *should* be constructed for them.

This is not to say that Marx was not also reflecting powerful forces in his own culture—of course he was, which makes him the great figure of history he is, rather than an obscure eccentric, complaining about his boils. It is only to say that the prism through which these forces were refracted was the person, Karl Marx, as I have tried to depict him page by page from the youthful poet to the mature revolutionary. The result was *his* vision of "reality," which, like that of a great painter or literary artist's, then imposed itself on millions of people as also being *their* reality.

X

A Conclusion
Without an End

Marx was a particular individual, responding to the circumstances of the Industrial Revolution and its surrounding culture and events. He sought to give meaning—his meaning—to the upheaval I have labeled as "axial." Initially, he attempted to do so as part of the 19th-century effort to move from religion to philosophy to social science. The model was the natural sciences, depicted especially by Auguste Comte (who, incidentally, first used the term "sociology" in his *Cours de philosophie positive* in 1837). In abolishing philosophy, Marx glimpsed the necessity of grounding its aspirations in reality, i.e., social-economic reality, but, I argue, he went astray by converting reality into revolution. At this point, in what might be referred to as "the return of the repressed," revolution turned into a secular version of religion.

In his own life, Marx went from being an accepting religious youth (unless we believe him to have been a hypocrite in this particular matter), to a law student, to a philosopher, and then to a journalist and revolutionary. His weapons as a revolutionary thinker were, first, critique, and then "science," i.e., social science. A young Marx, with a human face, and an old Marx, with Stalin-like features, are often aligned with the two modes of his thought (in my view, however, the youthful critique prepares the way for Marx's social science, and is never dispensed with).

What did Marx actually know about the natural sciences, the supposed model at the time for the social sciences? The evidence is very thin. We may recall that his Gymnasium leaving certificate states that he had a good knowledge of mathematics, but only "moderate" knowledge in physics. More important than any specific scientific knowledge is what we may call the "philosophy of science," i.e., insight into the real nature and procedure of the natural sciences. Here there is simply no evidence that Marx ever thought seriously about the matter. Where there is constant examination by his contemporary, Darwin, concerning the role of observation, theory, verification, etc., there is no hint of any such preoccupation in Marx.

As it happens, the natural sciences are not a particularly useful model for the social sciences, where the phenomena under observation—man and society—are significantly different in kind from that with which natural science is concerned, and where crucial experimentation is usually not possible. Without going into details in this complex subject, aside from what was said in the previous chapter, the irony is that Marx was not particularly handicapped by his lack of reflection on the real nature of the natural sciences. Marx resembles men such as Vico or Hegel, whose superficial if not wrong understanding of the natural sciences nevertheless (or therefore?) yielded pioneering insights into the nature of the human or social sciences. Marx then joined to this tradition a tendency to "scientism," i.e., pseudo-science; in this he was like many of his contemporaries working in the social sciences.

19th-century natural science, too, had emerged from philosophy. Indeed, until the middle of the 1800s, men like Faraday still preferred to call themselves "natural philosphers," as Newton had done in the 1700s. Professionalization into physicists, chemists, and biologists was a correspondent characteristic of the specialization attendant on the industrial revolution. A similar movement was changing philosophy into social science (though Marx did not favor that term), with the latter, in turn, beginning to break up in the 1860s into the specializations of anthropology, sociology, political science (as a profession), and, somewhat earlier, economics; and Marx was at the forefront of the initial part of the movement.

Without formal designation, but as part of his overall schema, Marx made contributions especially to the theory of what we today call sociology: theories about social stratification, the sociology of knowledge, the dynamics of social change, etc. His ideas about alienation, about class and the proletariat, about technology and industry, about capitalism and economic development, and about the relation of theory to practice offer powerful insights. Although many scholars esteem Marx for his economics—and perceive it to be his prime contribution—what he really offers is sociological in nature. In seeking to analyze the reality of industrial society and its attendant phenomena, Marx produced ways of conceptualizing it that still guide and inform us today. Some of the most exciting work by recent historians, for example, has been by neo-Marxists, inspired by his ideas and theories, as they write on the rise of capitalism, the world market, the working class, the modern political revolutions, and so forth. Indeed, as I remarked earlier, even non-Marxists, or anti-Marxists, operate, in part, in his terms, even if only in reaction.

With this said, and due acknowledgment given to Marx's contributions to modern social science, something more must be added. Marxism, as I have been arguing, is not the same thing as particular Marxist theories. The latter can be taken and used separately, they can be handled critically, and they can be superseded readily, i.e., they can be regarded as theories in social science. Marxism, on the other hand, is a whole, a world view, which, on closer inspection, turns out to be a new "religion." It is a dogma, which, while open to challenge on "theological" grounds, is accepted "on the whole" by the faithful, and used to order and guide their lives. There can be no free inquiry in such a "religion," for it serves other purposes than the pursuit of scientific knowledge.

If the parts are contributions to social science, and useful in that endeavor, the totality is a matter of political faith. There are followers, but no worshippers, of sociologists such as Max Weber or Emile Durkheim; Marx has both. He sought not only to understand reality—the industrial world—but to change it. In the process, Marx's analysis turned into an eschatology, for the change he wished—revolution—needed the passions of religious faith and hope to fuel it, rather than the cold touch of social science. The claim to "science," as I have stressed, is a modern form of "religious" appeal. Marx wanted, most fundamentally, not only to change existing society, but to construct a new world, a new Eden, which would be closer to the innermost aspirations of his heart and psyche.

II

The problem in the social sciences of reconciling "what is" with "what should be" is illustrated by a comparison of Adam Smith and Marx on the question of equality. On moral grounds one could argue that equality is an obviously good thing. On practical grounds, one could contend that, although certain kinds of equality can be and should be approached—equality under the law, freedom of expression, equality of political representation, etc.—full and total equality (whatever that would mean) cannot be achieved; and that the effort to achieve it will, in fact, lead to tyranny and greater inequality of various kinds. All of these points, needless to say, are open to further definition and argument—philosophers will argue whether, morally, equality is *prima facie* a good thing, political scientists, whether it is or is not achievable—but, I hope, the general problem with which I am trying to deal is clear.

Now, Smith, in his *Lectures on Jurisprudence* (1762–63 and 1766), defended the "usefull inequality in the fortunes of mankind which naturally and necessarily arises from the various degrees of capacity, industry, and diligence in the different individuals." His argument was that the single-minded pursuit of equality undercuts motivation, and therefore reduces, in its effect, the standard of living. It is only on the basis of inequality, rooted as it is in man's nature, that, according to Smith, the ordinary day laborer "has more of the conveniences and luxuries of life than an Indian prince at the head of 1000 naked savages" (in *The Wealth of Nations*, he changed this to an African king, at the head of 10,000), i.e., Smith is asserting that the productive affluence of modern commercial society is a result of the drive that exists in a competitive economy permitting inequality. In turn, inequality of fortune introduces regular government; or, as Smith says, "Till there be property there can be no government."[1] In short, government is instituted for the protection of private property, which is the underpinning of inequality.

Marx takes the opposite position. Inequality is morally indefensible and, in any case, not useful; in the long run, it fetters productive activity. Rather than enriching the day laborer, it exploits and impoverishes him, while alienating him from his product. Marx, like Smith, agrees that government is to protect property, but Marx wishes to do away with both.

Where in this argument are we able to decide "what is"—mainly a social science question?—and bring to bear on it the possible, realizable "what should be," primarily an ethical or religious question? Marx himself took it as a given that equality was a desired good (in fact, he went beyond ordinary equality and proclaimed, "From each according to his ability, to each according to his need"). He made no effort to study for himself the meaning or nuances of equality, nor its consequences, as did Tocqueville in *Democracy in America* (which Marx read) or John Stuart Mill in *On Liberty.* Instead, Marx operated mostly by definition, critique, and millennial longing. The mix of social science and eschatology in his work, therefore, is often hard to disentangle.

Some sociologists writing after Marx, such as Robert Michels and Gaetano Mosca, have argued for an "iron law of oligarchy": all complex societies, including a communist one, will necessarily end up in a pyramidal distribution of authority, because communication, and therefore power, necessarily goes from top to bottom, whether in a Marxist trade union or a capitalist corporation. Leaders and elites, on this account, will always be with us, whatever the property arrangements made in a particular society.[2]

Such a critique of Marx tries to join the issue on a sociological basis. Its proponents would further argue that any complex social structure requires authority, and such authority must wrap itself, even if only modestly, in the veil of mystification. Man, according to this view (Burke, for example, would be a proponent), cannot live by bread alone, but requires illusions. Marx, on the other hand, devoted much of his work, to lifting the "veil." He wished to expose bourgeois reality, to demystify it. In doing so, he was only doing what bourgeois *philosophes* had done to feudalism's claims. (Even Max Weber argues that modern bourgeois science is emptying the world of its mystery, and leaving man in an "iron cage.") The question remains, however, can Communist society, *as a society,* remain functional and intact without its own mystification? Is some sort of "religion," or ideology, necessary to bind men together in a society?

Marx's answer seems to be that, once the "cash nexus" is dissolved and private property done away with, man will be connected to man by love alone. In this respect, the humanist Marx appears to persist, importantly, into the "scientific" Marx. Politics and power, based as they are solely on inequality of property, will, according to Marx, disappear in the face of man's natural good feelings.

III

I have already discussed Marx's position as a psychologist—his insights, or lack thereof, into man's nature—in the previous chapter. His psychological views are, of course, connected to his sociological observations, and both related to the "what should be" and "what is" problem. Now I need to relate these parts of Marx to his work as historian. Much has been written recently by scholars on this subject, and it will not be easy to untangle Marx's views here, for they were neither uniform nor simple.

The overall context for his attitudes was the state of historical thought in 19th-century Germany, and especially Hegel's influence. Hegel, in his *Philosophy of History*, had, as one scholar puts it succinctly, "subordinated history to a pretentious metaphysical system and had claimed for it a scientific character."[3] Among historians *per se*, Leopold von Ranke called for a *Weltgeschichte*, which would show empirically—for Ranke rejected Hegel's metaphysical approach—the way history moved to the fulfillment of a higher purpose (in this case, as Ranke's pupils endeavored to demonstrate, the enlargement of the German state and its cultural supremacy).

Together, though with different emphases, Hegel and Ranke dominated German historiography, and drove it toward a belief that history was predetermined, linear (although with ups and downs), and progressive, i.e., here to reveal God or Reason's purpose on earth (which coincided with the mission of Germany and its "great men"). Opposed to this view was the one upheld, for example, by Jacob Burckhardt, who believed that history was, indeed, a process guided by general laws—i.e., not mere chaos—but that such laws were to be derived from experience and not as deductions from metaphysical assumptions. Moreover, culture had its own life and was an independent variable.

Where did Marx stand in this discussion? In a comprehensive article, Walter Adamson, building on the scholarship of Helmut Fleischer, sums up the abundant literature on the subject and argues that Marx adopted four separate historical approaches in the course of his work.[4] One approach is anthropological, where history is seen as "the playing-out of a 'process of humanization' which is inherent in the 'nature of the human species' itself." Here Marx assumes a human "essence," which exists before any specific form of socioeconomic activity; history is its preordained realization. This approach to history characterizes Marx's work up to 1844. A second approach is pragmatalogical, where history is seen empirically, but where generalizations can be drawn from the record of man's actual efforts to fulfill his "needs" (whose fulfillment gives rise to new needs). Marx was inspired in this approach by the empirical work of Engels (whom he had met in Paris, as we remember, in 1844). This approach was the dominant one in Marx's work up until the 1850s. A third approach is nomological, where history is regarded "as a natural process taking place in accordance with definite laws"; the laws are based on "the logic of objective historical structures and processes." This is the Marx of the *Critique of Political Economy* (1859), and later of *Capital* (1867), analyzing civil society with the aid of theories from political economy. A fourth approach is historiographic, where Marx is concerned with the relation of history as a mode of inquiry to the events themselves. The outcome of his reflections is a view that history is not something whose outcome can be predicted because it is based on "laws" given from the outset; rather, we must start from the present, in order to understand the genesis and development of history itself. This approach, which is Adamson's particular addition to Fleischer, is to be found only in Marx's *Grundrisse* (1857).

As we can see, the subject is a complicated one, with many nuances and subtleties of interpretation involved. Marx's intellectual development was convoluted, and its results were not always consistently deployed. We can glimpse, however, some important implications for our general inquiry peeping through this arcane discussion of Marx's approaches to history.

Marx was clearly involved in a delicate balancing act of parts of his intellectual heritage, i.e., in this case, the context of historical thought in 19th-century Germany, with overlaps to be found among the four approaches outlined above, as well as deep differences comingled. Adamson thinks the pragmatological and nomological are variants of one view and are to be distinguished from the anthropological view. All three, however, weave in and out of Marx's writings, and Adamson is helpful when he says, "All too often . . . studies assume uncritically that all of Marx's mature economic writings must have been based on a single historical and historiographical outlook. No doubt this assumption derives, at least in part, from the long standing tendency among Marx interpreters to comprehend his intellectual development in terms of 'early' and 'late' phases. Whatever changes there were in his views are understood to be between phases and not within them. Yet, as we have seen here, the actual development of Marx's historical views was considerably more complex."[5]

If this is true in regard to Marx's historical outlook, it is also true in regard to the other facets of his work and character. There does seem to be an important shift of sorts around 1844–46, but the division into an early and late, a young and old, a humanist and scientific Marx is, as I too have argued, too reductive of his actual unified complexity.

With this point accepted, we can look again at the four approaches to history in terms of some of the issues which we have been discussing earlier. The anthropological approach coincides with an early, eschatological Marx. The pragmatological approach reminds us of Burckhardt's position, and points to the sociological Marx. The nomological approach also accords with the sociological Marx, but now appears to link up with the immanent laws of development assumed in the anthropological approach; the difference is that what was a metaphysically justified eschatology in the latter takes on a "scientific" form in the former. I have referred to this aspect of Marx as his "secular religion." The historiographic approach is neither metaphysically or scientistically eschatological, but a more refined and thoughtful version of the pragmatological. If history is a social science, Marx was offering an "internal" version of scientific methodology, i.e., one in which general laws, if they exist, are derived from the events themselves and not imposed on them from the outside, because of metaphysical requirements. Put forth in 1857 in the *Grundrisse*, the historiographic approach was submerged by the nomological, eschatological needs of Marx's revolutionary character and aspirations. The conflict in Marx's historical approaches, just as in his sociological and psychological theories, was in his heart and psyche as well as in his mind.

IV

It is time to return to the beginning. I have tried to portray "Marx with a Human Face." His humanity expresses itself in his life and work (as his humanity is also sometimes repressed in them, or altered in its appearance). What survives of Marx are his theoretical and polemical writings plus the documentary evidence—ranging from his own letters to contemporary reminiscences—of his personal existence. It is from these taken together that we derive our understanding of him and his theories, and can interpret Marxism in relation to its creator, Marx.

Our first problem is, necessarily, with the texts. I have already suggested the difficulties involved: what if certain texts didn't exist? What if others suddenly appeared? For example, Adamson speaks of Marx's historiographic approach, which appears in the *Grundrisse* and nowhere else. This was a hefty manuscript which Marx worked on in 1857–58 in preparation for the writing of the *Critique of Political Economy* and *Capital* but never published in his lifetime. It first saw publication in 1939–41, edited in Moscow, with the title *Grundrisse der Kritik der Politischen Okonomie* (some small extracts had appeared in 1903 in a German periodical) and drew almost no attention until 1953, when it was republished in Berlin. Without the late appearance of this text, we would not know about the "historiographic" Marx.

Once available, it helps us to understand Marx in a new way. In its light, we can go back and look at the other texts, able now to place them in a larger context. Marx's meaning becomes clearer and deeper for us. Similarly, for example, in order to understand and evaluate his secular religion, we have to comprehend Marx's psychological commitments and know precisely where he fell short in his knowledge of human nature. Such an understanding does not come solely from the reading of the texts; it requires us to understand Marx himself—which is why we must know the text of his life; and why it matters who Karl Marx was. The discovery of yet another unpublished Marxist text—another *Grundrisse*—would again cause us to reinterpret Marx, and thus Marxism (for the latter, too, would be reinterpreted in the light of the new revelations). Indeed, as things now stand, many of the most important parts of the corpus, ranging from the *Economic and Philosophical Manuscripts of 1844* through *The German Ideology* to the *Grundrisse*, and Engels's edition of the second and third volumes of *Capital*, were unpublished during Marx's life.

Obviously, what was unpublished (and therefore tantamount to unknown) could have little influence on Marxism, as a movement, while Marx lived, except as informing and speaking through the published works. Yet, if we wish to know the meaning of Marxism, we must also read these works, once published, and give them the same attention as the published ones. In them, we first really see, for example, the true lineaments of a "humanist" Marx as well as an "historiographic" one.

In their light, we suddenly feel better able to understand the depth of both Marx's meaning and his appeal to his readers. Close textual analysis, of *all* the texts, reveals the "real" Marx.

The same is true of his life. The life informs the texts, published and unpublished. It was a real person, Karl Marx, and not some spectre, who wrote Marx's works. He "meant" something in these works. To understand Marx's meaning, on all its levels, we need to analyze and understand his life, just as if it, too, were a text; we need to analyze it within the context of the written texts, going back and forth from one to the other.

It is this that I have tried to do. I started with Marx, the school boy and the youthful poet, for this is where our documentary evidence— works and life—begins for all practical purposes, i.e., is available. I then sought to follow the course of his development, personal and professional, biographical and intellectual, as he experienced it. Our evidence is, naturally, the texts which are available to us, as I have described them, with each new piece of evidence, properly evaluated and interpreted, shedding light on every other piece.

I have argued that it does make a difference that it was Karl Marx, and not someone else, who created Marxism. Marxism is a hybrid of many things, but especially of one man's secular religious response to the Industrial Revolution, mixed with a social scientific analysis of that axial event; and his social science itself reflects the tension involved in fusing "what should be" with "what is." To this hybrid, this potent synthesis, is added the passion of Marx's prose, with form giving life to content. Marxist theories, consequently, are not like theories in natural science—Einstein's relativity theory—whose verification (or lack of refutation) can be undertaken independently of its creator and his feelings. They are, rather, more like Thoreau's philosophy of how to live, though with a strong addition of social science; in theories of this kind, a simple, "Do as I say, not what I do," does not suffice. As children know, the "what I do" does matter; and it matters in the case not only of a Thoreau but, even more importantly, in the case of a Marx.

V

Marx, I have argued, as the founder of the great modern secular religion of Marxism, can be seen in the clear daylight of historical evidence and analysis. His face is human, not god-like (though many of his followers have tried to deify him). His life is a real life, developing, as all real lives do, out of a unique combination of natural endowment and social environment; and it is as part of that real, human life that he wrote his works and played out his role as a revolutionary.

By looking at his life and works together, and analyzing them carefully, a number of paradoxes in Marxism can be explained; and a number of double meanings can be illuminated and understood. Indeed, it is the ambiguities of Marxism, stemming as they do from Marx himself, that give the doctrine much of its power.

There is, first, and foremost, the rejection of religion as such—in the name of a new "religion." The roots of this seeming paradox are in the details of young Karl's own religious background—his Christian-Jewish heritage—as I have tried to show, combined with his intellectual absorption in Hegel and the critique of religion (where Judaism and capitalism become conflated), and further combined with the need of a "religious" response to the Industrial Revolution to clothe itself in the garments of "science."

The next paradox is that Marx is more a Romantic than a real scientist. As a Romantic, he might be expected to share in the feelings of a Wordsworth or a Keats, who saw science as threatening and dehumanizing (although Shelley did not). As Wordsworth remarked, "We murder to dissect." Instead, Marx the Romantic dealt with the threat of science in an opposite manner from Wordsworth, subverting it to his own purposes. Thus, outwardly, he glorified science and claimed that his own work was scientific. A deeper look, I suggest, shows that Marx was fundamentally unscientific, if not anti-scientific; his Thoreau-like idyll of a communist society in which man hunts, fishes, and criticizes seems to have little room for the laboratory worker, and his vague utopian stateless community, built though it is on the result of the dialectic of changes in the tools underlying productive relations, affords no possibility of future changes in technology, and therefore in society.

There is also the paradox of Marx who, rejecting the "wealth of nations" in favor of internationalism, nevertheless became the inspiration for nationalist revolution. I suggest that in spite of his renunciation of his German (specifically Prussian) citizenship, and his subsequent lifelong exile, Marx, was, in the deepest sense, a German nationalist. It was the German bourgeoisie who inspired his disdain. It was in Germany that he first hoped for a communist revolution (see the Critique of Hegel's *Philosophy of Right*). We see the conflicted nature of his feelings in what he wrote to Engels in 1867 upon the completion of the first volume of *Capital*. "You must understand, my dear fellow, that there must be many shortcomings in detail in a work like mine. But the *composition*, the overall structure, is a triumph of German science, something an individual German can avow since it is in no way *his* merit, but belongs more to the *nation*. All the more happily, since otherwise it is the *silliest nation* under the sun."[6] Overtly anti-nationalist, Marx's "German" nationalist attachments and concerns breathed through his writings, whatever he might say, and later followers took up the "doing" in their own nationalist revolutions, e.g., in Russia and China.

What about the Marx who, wishing to abolish the division of labor, and consequently intellectuals as such, spent his whole life as an intellectual, and, more importantly, created a Marxism which legitimizes the role of an elite? Is this a mere unintended consequence, a distortion of Marx? Or another instance of the "do as I say" situation? Did Marx's own life, his dictatorial character, belie his own words? If one can't act according to one's own "I say," how, realistically, can one expect others to do so? In any case, the paradox remains of Marx the anti-intellectual spawning a new "mandarin" class.

We must also deal with the Marx who, accused of egotism by his father, dedicated his life to the service of mankind. The parental injunctions and admonitions placed Marx in a double bind. He, who acknowledged feelings of self-contempt, became a supreme egotist, who drowned his own, and the bourgeoisie's egoism, in the icy waters of revolutionary asceticism. The result was, in fact, that Marx could and did offer solace and hope to the victims of the Industrial Revolution. He held out for them a vision of a world "beyond self," in which, nevertheless, "self" would expand and become freed of any dependency.

This vision itself takes us to the last paradox. In it, Marx combined the deepest aspirations of his soul: his longings for "endless strife," constant exhibition of strength and manliness, and triumphant final struggle to achieve communism, and then, once that state is achieved, a cessation of all conflict, and an end to all aggression and "embitterment." We are left, finally, with a deeply upsetting appeal: Marx calls out from the depths of his own ambivalent soul to the echoing ambivalent "feelings" of our own; and then leaves us as well with a double bind, for he is calling us to hate and then enjoining us, magically, to love.

It is, I would assert, a black-white exhortation, an echo of the demonic–

god-like (Promethean) struggle in Marx himself, which offers at one and the same time a profound expression and understanding of human nature and the workings of society—which is partly why it is so successful as a revolutionary appeal—and an equally profound ignorance. As a result, we are left with a real world that echoes Marx's youthful poetry, where he spoke of a world which he would "destroy for ever"; once destroyed, however, he feared that he could "create no world" to take its place, or at least not one of love and harmony. Mankind, it would appear, in spite of Marx's Promethean attempt, is condemned to go on cycling through the universe of its passions and thoughts, as well as his, "World without end."

Epilogue

Marx and Marxism gives us a heightened awareness that an ideology—
a secular religion—is a vital part of any society. As part of his particular
ideology, Marx stressed the way in which a society's ethos and values
are *created* by its members. This awareness is now part of our consciousness. Although Marx did not see his own work as ideological, that
very work, paradoxically, forces us to recognize it as such. In turn, that
recognition makes it subject to the same kind of critique, or criticism,
applied to capitalism by Marx himself.

Marx was a great creative battler, always striving for a better world.
Nothing was sacred for him, nothing curtailed his desire to perceive the
human condition clearly and to act on that perception. The truest honor
we can accord him is to carry on in his spirit. To do so is to realize that
Marxism, as a doctrine, an ideology, is outmoded. It is largely irrelevant
to our contemporary problems. Its economic analysis is anachronistic,
as is its appeal to class conflict. It offers pious simplicities, where our
problems are complex. (I hasten to add that the same can be said of
capitalist ideology, in its dogmatic forms; the present book is, however,
only inferentially a book about capitalism.)[1]

Marxism, in its various forms, i.e., national embodiments, varies
greatly: the Yugoslav version is not the same as the Russian, nor is the
Chinese the same as the Ethiopian. We have noted the paradox of in-

ternational Marxism fueling nationalist revolutions. Marx had correctly called attention to the breakdown of affective ties in economic life under capitalism—the cash nexus was the only one remaining that he recognized—but neglected the other ties that contrived to hold people together: religious, ethnic, communal, *and* nationalistic. In fact, Marxism itself as secular or civil religion gave a valid content to new nationalisms, supplying a source of unity to former African tribal kingdoms as well as to ancient celestial ones, such as the Chinese. It is these national Marxisms that comprise what we call "Marxism," and which vary so greatly, while still sharing, to greater or lesser degree, the simplicities of the overarching ideology.

There is a slogan current today: "Better dead than Red." For those who hold to this view, Communism is a monstrous evil, a world in the hands of the Devil. Rather than "live" under such conditions, violent anti-Marxists would prefer to bring the world crashing down on all our heads. I hope that my book contributes to dispelling such a simple-minded notion. Whatever the flaws in Marxism, it still remains a *human*, not inhuman, creation, with the potentiality for creating viable cultures. Opposition to it should not cause us to overlook this fact. Marxism is not evil incarnate, but one among a number of current ways of organizing human societies.

With this said, I can return to my statement that it is outmoded. The fact is that we are confronted with problems that go well beyond the quarrels of capitalism and communism. We appear to have a cluster of world-wide problems that has created a special crisis of human survival: overpopulation, depletion of resources, pollution, and, overwhelming all else, nuclear holocaust. Human will, guided by good will, and critical understanding—these are the essentials needed to deal with the challenge. Capitalism and communism, locked in ideological conflict, are largely irrelevant to this challenge; the problems transcend both, and require a truly dialectical "uplifting."

Let us perform a thought experiment. Imagine the United States as a communist state. Would this end conflict and solve the problems? A glance at the Soviet Union's relations to Poland or Yugoslavia shatters any such optimism. Let us imagine the reverse: Russia becomes capitalistic. A glance at history shows that capitalist nations have entered into wars and conflicts with each other, too. There is no simple solution.

Capitalism and communism must, for the time being, co-exist if humanity is to exist. At some point, as a result of having to cope with the problems now facing the world, both will fade into some other social system. Mao's comment to Edgar Snow in 1965 is farseeing. As Snow reported: "Mao's voice dropped away and he half closed his eyes. Man's condition on this earth was changing with ever increasing rapidity. A thousand years from now all of us, he said, even Marx, Engels, and Lenin would probably appear rather ridiculous. . . ."[2]

Mao's prescient view is *sub specie aeternitatis.* Meanwhile, we must cope with our present reality. Détente, co-existence, whatever one may call it, is the order of the day. It should not be grudging, hostile, and constantly seeking to achieve a competitive advantage; but, rather, carried out in a spirit of mutuality, recognizing in the opponent a "human" quality. In the wise words of Erik Erikson, "For the only alternative to armed competition seems to be the effort to *activate in the historical partner what will strengthen him in his historical development even as it strengthens the actor in his own development—toward a common future identity.*"[3]

I have written this book in that spirit. Marx's meaning is a human one—his own favorite maxim was that "Nothing human is alien to me"—and calls for a human response. His is a great creative effort, however open to criticism and rejection in its dogmatic form. Marxists and non-Marxists alike need to reexamine Marx in the light of the realities that history—meaning ourselves—has created since his time. We must all recognize the mote in our own eyes and the way it blinds us to "what actually is." We must also reexamine the inner reality—the "what should be"—that we bring to this task. Marx, that great creative spirit with carbuncles, places this enterprise forcefully before us as he wrestles with the tension between his desire for what I have called a religious ending and his drive for a critical, or analytic, understanding and solution to the industrial crisis of his time. We, in our time, with our crisis, must wrestle as mightily as he did. This is the final meaning inhering in the life and work of Karl Marx.

Chronology of Karl Marx, 1818–1883

1818   (May 5) Karl Marx born at Trier, Prussia (in the Rhineland), to Heinrich and Henriette (Pressburg) Marx.

1824   Karl and siblings baptized in Protestant faith (father previously baptized in 1816).

1825   Mother baptized.

1830–35   Karl studies in Trier gymnasium (high school).

1834   Heinrich gives constitutionalist speech in a political club, attracting suspicion of the government.

1835   Karl takes *Abitur*, and writes school leaving essays; in October enters University of Bonn, law faculty.

1836   Becomes engaged to Jenny von Westphalen in the summer; in October transfers to University of Berlin, law faculty. Writes poetry and other literary fragments, works feverishly into next year on studies in law, philosophy, history, and English and Italian languages.

1837   Letter to his father.

1838   Father dies.

1839–41   Karl studies Greek philosophy and writes doctoral dissertation, *The Difference Between the Democritean and Epicurean Philosophies of*

Nature. In 1841, receives Ph.D. from University of Jena. Moves to Bonn to work with Bruno Bauer, hoping to secure a teaching post there.

1842   Abandons idea of university teaching; begins to write about censorship and citizenship for Young Hegelian *Deutsche Jahrbücher* and for an opposition newspaper, the *Rheinische Zeitung*. Becomes editor of latter in October, moves to Cologne. Baron von Westphalen, Jenny's father and Karl's "second father," dies. In November, first meeting with Engels, who stops by on way to England.

1843   Resigns as editor of *Rheinische Zeitung* over censorship issue, arranges to leave Germany and work with Arnold Ruge on *Deutsch-Französische Jahrbücher* in Paris. Marries Jenny (June 19) and honeymoons in Kreuznach. Write "On the Jewish Question" and "Contributions to the Critique of Hegel's *Philosophy of Right*: Introduction" for *Jahrbücher*.

1844   Writes *Economic and Philosophic Manuscripts*. Double issue of *Jahrbücher*, edited by Marx and Ruge, published in Paris; includes Engels's "Outlines of a Critique of Political Economy," as well as Marx's two articles written in 1843. Returning from Manchester, England, to Germany, Engels, for the second time, meets Marx in Paris. Beginning of their life-long collaboration.

On May 1, daughter Jenny born.

1845   Banished from Paris by French government, Marx moves to Brussels. *Holy Family* (written with Engels) published. Marx also writes "Theses on Feuerbach." Engels joins him in Brussels, and two of them take six week trip to England (to study economics).

Daughter Laura born.

Marx renounces Prussian citizenship.

1845–46   Marx and Engels write *The German Ideology*.

Begin organized correspondence with communists throughout Europe.

1846   Son Edgar born.

1847   Marx writes *Poverty of Philosophy*. He and Engels help organize German Workers' Society. Both Marx and Engels take part in Second Congress of the Communist League, in London. Begin work on *Communist Manifesto* for League. In December, Marx, in Brussels, gives lectures later published as *Wage Labor and Capital* (1849).

1848   *Manifesto* published. Marx expelled from Brussels, moves to Paris and then Cologne, to support revolution. In Cologne, helps publish *Neue Rheinische Zeitung.*

1849   Marx tried for subversion in Cologne, but his speeches convince jury to let him off. But expelled from Prussia, and *Neue Rheinische Zeitung* folds, Marx losing about 7,000 thaler. After going to Southern Germany and then Paris to aid the revolution, goes to London, where he will spend rest of his life.

Son Guido born.

1850   Marx takes up studies in British Museum. Supported by Engels, who works for the family firm in Manchester. Marx publishes *The Class Struggles in France.*

Destitute, thrown out of home, Marxes move to small flat in Soho quarter.

Son Guido dies.

1851   Marx accepts job as regular contributor to New York Daily Tribune (most of the articles written by Engels).

Daughter Franceska born (March).

Birth of Frederick Demuth (June), Marx's illegitimate son with Lenchen, but Engels named as the father.

1852   Marx's *The Eighteenth Brumaire of Louis Bonaparte* published.

Daughter Franceska dies.

1855   Daughter Eleanor born.

Son Edgar dies; Marx very depressed, Jenny sick.

1856   Jenny inherits money from mother; Marxes able to move to more wholesome housing.

1857–58   Marx works on major ideas for his magnum opus on economic and social theory (to be published after his death as *Grundrisse* [1939–41]).

A seventh child born, but dies immediately.

1859   *A Contribution to the Critique of Political Economy* published.

1860   *Herr Vogt* published.

1861   Visits Germany to get money from relatives, and meets with Ferdinand Lassalle, who is organizing German workers.

1861–63   Marx writing *Theories of Surplus Value* (unpublished until later).

1863   Death of Mary Burns, Engels's mistress; Marx fails to offer condolences, offending Engels.

Lassalle organizes *Allgemeine Deutsche Arbeiterverein*, the first effective German socialist party.

Marx's mother, Henriette, dies, leaving him a small legacy.

1864   Founding of International Working Men's Association in London.

Wilhelm Wolff, close follower of Marx, dies, leaving him a small legacy. Also, death of Lassalle.

1864–71   Marx active in affairs of General Council of the International. Marked by struggles with followers of Bakunin and Proudhon.

1867   *Capital*, Vol. I, published (Vols. II and III, though mostly completed at this date, only published posthumously, edited by Engels).

1871   Marx writes *The Civil War in France*. Works in support of Paris Commune.

1872   First International effectively ended.

1875   *Critique of the Gotha Program.*

1881   Wife Jenny dies.

1883   Daughter Jenny Longuet dies, followed by death of Karl Marx (March 14).

Notes

INTRODUCTION

1. I owe this particular example to Joseph Weizenbaum, *Computer Power and Human Reason* (San Francisco: W. H. Freeman and Co., 1976).

I. WHY MARX?

1. As of 1982, adherents of the world religions, as given in *The World Almanac and Book of Facts* (New York: Newspaper Enterprise Association, 1983), are as follows:

Christian (all denominations)	997,783,140
(Of these the largest is the	
Roman Catholic with 580,061,800)	
Muslim	592,157,900
Hindu	481,241,300
Buddhist	256,387,200
The total for all religions is:	2,585,050,410
(i.e., larger than the Marxist,	
though no single religion is	
as large)	

A rough estimate, derived from *The Yearbook on International Communist Affairs*, 1983 (Stanford: Hoover Institution Press, 1983) of Communist Party members worldwide is 77,873,000. This, of course, does not give us the figures for Marxist "followers" in general, which I estimate, however, to be between 1.5 and 2 billion.

2. I do not claim originality for viewing Marxism as a "secular religion"; it is my use in which originality hopefully adheres. The term itself, presumably, was first employed by the German sociologist, Edward Spranger. Or so says Jules Monnerot, in his important, though overly polemical work, *The Sociology of Communism* (London: G. Allen and Unwin, 1953 [original French 1949]). Nicholas Berdiaev, the Russian philosopher, wrote in the 1920s about Bolshevism as a messianic ideology, complete with sacred books and a concept of the chosen, aiming at salvation, etc. Among the more modern books that treat Marxism as a religious and mythical system, the most penetrating is Robert Tucker, *Philosophy and Myth in Karl Marx* (Cambridge: Cambridge University Press, 1961).

3. Karl Jaspers, *The Origin and Goal of History*, trans. M. Bullock (London: Routledge, Kegan and Paul, 1953 [orig. 1949]).

4. The best books on the first Industrial Revolution are Phyllis Deane, *The First Industrial Revolution* (Cambridge: Cambridge University Press, 1965); David S. Landes, *The Unbound Prometheus* (Cambridge: Cambridge University Press, 1969); E.J. Hobsbawm, *Industry and Empire* (New York: Pantheon Books, 1968); and T.S. Ashton, *The Industrial Revolution: 1760–1830* (London: Oxford University Press, 1948), which, though outdated, is still a useful short account.

5. Cf. Carl Becker, *The Heavenly City of the Eighteenth-Century Philosophers* (New Haven: Yale University Press, 1932).

6. M.H. Abrams, *Natural Supernaturalism* (New York: W.W. Norton & Co., 1977), p. 65. The quotes that follow are on p. 66 and pp. 62–63. Marx, in a letter to Arnold Ruge, 27 April 1842, refers to an article he had written, "On the Romantics," which might have given us more insight into Marx's own feelings about the subject (*Karl Marx Frederick Engels: Collected Works*, 50 vols. [New York: International Publishers, 1975–], I, 387; hereafter cited as MECW). Unfortunately, the article was not published, and the manuscript seems to have disappeared. For another view of the importance of romanticism in Marx's thought, see Leszek Kolakowski, *Main Currents of Marxism: Its Rise, Growth, and Dissolution*, 3 vols. (Oxford: Clarendon Press, 1978), I, 408–412.

7. Karl Marx, *Capital*, trans. by Eden Paul and Cedar Paul (London: J.M. Dent and Sons), I, 392–93. In a letter to Ferdinand Lassalle, Marx added rather superciliously, "Darwin's writing is very important and fits in quite conveniently for me as the natural science basis for the historical struggle. One has to take into account of course the unrefined [*grob*] English manner of development." Marx then added, "Despite all the shortcomings, it is the first time that teleology in the natural sciences has been given not only the death blow, but that the rational meaning of it has been expounded empir-

ically" (16 January 1861, Karl Marx and Friedrich Engels, *Werke*, [East Berlin: Institute for Marxism-Leninism, 1956ff], XXX, 578; hereafter cited as MEW).

Interestingly, Engels had written Marx two years earlier, in 1859, as follows: "Incidentally, Darwin, which I am reading right now, is quite fantastic. Teleology in one respect had not been destroyed, and that has happened now. Moreover, there has not been up to now such a wonderful attempt to show evidence of historical development in nature, and never before with such success. One has to take into account of course the clumsy [*plumpe*] English method" (12 December 1859, *Marx-Engels Briefwechsel*, 4 vols. [Berlin: Dietz Verlag, 1949], II, 547) In the original, Engels's passage reads, "Die plumpe englishe Methode muss man natürlich in den Kauf nehmen," and Marx's "Die grob englishe Manier der Entwicklung muss man natürlich mit in den kauf nehmen." Marx appears to have had an unusual memory.

For the actual relations between Marx and Darwin and Marx's intention to dedicate the English translation of *Capital* to Darwin, see Ralph Colp, Jr., "The Contacts Between Karl Marx and Charles Darwin," *Journal of the History of Ideas*, 35, No. 2 (January–March 1974).

8. I must thank my friend Fred Weinstein for pushing me to spell out our agreements and disagreements in this manner. This paragraph, in fact, reflects points he made to me in a private communication. The paragraph that follows reflects where we part company.

9. For a further explanation of why Marxism appealed to China, and the way in which the Russian experience both differed from the Chinese and yet set an example for it, see Stephen Andors, *China's Industrial Revolution* (New York: Pantheon Books, 1977), especially Chapters 1 and 2.

10. John Maynard Keynes, *The General Theory of Employment, Interest, and Money* (London: Macmillan & Co., 1964), p. 383.

11. Quoted in Richard Curt Kraus, *Class Conflict in Chinese Socialism* (New York: Columbia University Press, 1981), p. 70.

12. Quoted in Joseph W. Esherick, "On the Restoration of Capitalism," *Modern China*, (January 1979), p. 54.

13. The classic work on Engels is Gustav Mayer, *Friedrich Engels* (London: Chapman & Hall, 1936); this translation is an abbreviated version of the original two-volume work. See also Stephen Marcus, *Engels, Manchester, and the Working Class* (New York: Random House, 1974). A new biography of Engels is badly needed. Terrell Carver's little book, *Engels* (New York: Hill & Wang, 1981) is mainly interpretive, but points in the right directions even if one disagrees with some of the interpretations. As for the question whether Marx was, indeed, the father of Marxism, some scholars prefer to give credit (or debit) to others for inventing "Marxism" as something distinct from Marx's work. For example, Maximilien Rubel awards

the palm to Engels, whom he sees as inadvertently distorting Marx's ideas into an ideology, which could then lend itself to the horrors of Stalin's Russia ("The 'Marx Legend', or Engels, Founder of Marxism," in *Rubel on Karl Marx: Five Essays*, ed. Joseph O'Malley and Keith Algozin [Cambridge: Cambridge University Press, 1981]). So, too, does Norman Levine, *The Tragic Deception: Marx Contra Engels* (Santa Barbara: Clio Books, 1975). Werner Blumenberg declares that "Marxism is not his [Karl Marx's] creation; the person chiefly responsible for this was Karl Kautsky" (*Portrait of Karl Marx*, trans. Douglas Scott [New York: Herder & Herder, 1972 (original German 1962)], p. 178). On a different tack, some scholars reject the term "Marxism" as vague, ambiguous, confusing, and misleading. See, for example, Z. A. Jordan, *The Evolution of Dialectical Materialism* (New York: St. Martin's Press, 1967), pp. ix–x. One can see what Rubel, Blumenberg, and Jordan are driving at—any set of ideas as it becomes caught up in a political or social movement takes on a new form as an "ism"—but to detach Marxism from Marx is, in my view, simply misguided (further, Marxism has changed significantly, not only after Marx, but after Engels, Kautsky, etc, just as Christianity has changed after Christ). Cf. Kolakowski, *Main Currents*, I, 2–3, who takes the same position as I do, opposite Rubel's.

14. For illustrations of Marx, a handy volume is Blumenberg, *Portrait*.

15. Isaiah Berlin, *Karl Marx* (London: Oxford University Press, 1939), p. 29.

16. One of the starting points of this debate is the Hungarian communist, Georg Lukács, *History and Class Consciousness*, trans. Rodney Livingstone (Cambridge, MA.: The MIT Press, 1971 [original 1923]), which stressed the influence of Hegel on Marx and the importance of the theme of alienation. (For an account of Lukács's tortuous attempt to remain true to his own insights and yet remain a loyal follower of Marxist-Leninism, see Morris Watnick, "Georg Lukacs: An Intellectual Biography," *Soviet Survey*, No. 24 [April–June 1958] and No. 25 [July–Sept. 1958.]) The Polish émigré philosopher, Leslek Kolakowski, has continued the inquiry into the humanist roots of Marx's thought in his probing and difficult work, *Main Currents of Marxism*, especially Vol. I, previously cited. In this magisterial work, he places Marx in the tradition of thinkers who seek to solve the problem of the contingency of human existence (see his Chapter 1) and discerns a Marx whose humanist *praxis* is different from Engels's naturalistic science, but still can lead to Leninist-Stalinism as a logical possibility, although not forming part of Marx's intention. Others, not necessarily East Europeans, who carry on the debate can also give us its flavor. For example, the French Marxist, Louis Althusser, in his *For Marx* (trans. Ben Brewster [London: The Penguin Press, 1969] [orig. 1966]), contends that there is a radical break between a humanistic and scientific Marx, and prefers the latter. In contrast, Maximilien Rubel, a scholar who is also a French Marxist, argues for the unity of Marx's thought and emphasizes the contin-

uing validity of his humanism, i.e., his ethical socialism, while deploring its betrayal by "Marxists," starting with Engels and running through Lenin to Stalin. An Israeli scholar, Schlomo Avineri, in his *The Social and Political Thought of Karl Marx* (Cambridge: Cambridge University Press, 1968) agrees with Rubel concerning the unity of Marx's thought, but nevertheless concludes, "Leninism would have been inconceivable without Marx" (p. 258). And so the debate goes on, generally in what sounds much like a theological mode.

II. THE POETIC PHILOSOPHER

1. For Marx's poetry, see MECW, Vol. I. An interesting treatment is William M. Johnston, "Karl Marx's Verse of 1836–1837 as a Foreshadowing of his Early Philosophy," *Journal of the History of Ideas*, 28, No. 2 (April–June 1967), which makes the point that Marx went beyond mere romantic commonplaces by voicing the conventional sentiments "with a fury that suggests rebellion of a starker sort than mere poetic *Weltschmerz*" (p. 267). So, too, Leonard P. Wessell, Jr., *Karl Marx, Romantic Irony and the Proletariat: Studies in the Mythopoetic Origins of Marxism* (Baton Rouge: Louisiana State University Press, 1979), which also has some useful translations.

2. For some chapters from "Scorpion and Felix" and scenes from "Oulanem," see MECW, pp. 616–632 and 588–607.

3. Heinrich Heine *Sämtliche Schriften*, 6 vols. (Munich: Hanser Verlag, 1971), IV, 578. I have used the translation in E. H. Carr, *Karl Marx: A Study in Fanaticism* (London: J. M. Dent and Sons, 1934), p. 24.

4. Ferdinand Freiligrath to Karl Marx, 28 February 1860 in Manfred Häckel, ed., *Freiligraths Briefwechsel Mit Marx Und Engels* (Berlin: Akademie Verlag, 1968) I, 137, quoted in Blumenberg, *Portrait* p. 134. See *Rubel on Karl Marx: Five Essays*, ed. Joseph O'Malley and Keith Algozin (Cambridge: Cambridge University Press, 1981), pp. 69–74, for a different interpretation of "party." According to Rubel, by "party" Marx meant the party of mankind, in which he served, and not a political party, which he led and to which everyone had to be subservient. This is an interesting interpretation, though, in fact, Rubel admits that Marx's usage of the term "party" was erratic and confusing for his disciples. I would add that, in practice, Marx tended to confuse the party of mankind with himself, and was intolerant of those who did not agree with this identification.

5. Quoted in Eugene Lunn, *Marxism and Modernism* (Berkeley: University of California Press, 1982), p. 22.

6. MECW, I, 733.

III. RELIGION AND THE CALL TO A VOCATION

1. The text may be found most easily in MECW, Vol. I.

2. Auguste Cornu, *Karl Marx et Friedrich Engels, Leur vie et leur oeuvre*, 4 vols. (Paris: Presses Universitaires de France, 1955), Vol. I, *Les Années d'enfance et de jeunesse, la gauche hegélienne, 1818/1820–1844*. In this classic account, Cornu takes a view of Marx's religious development different from the one I am offering; see especially p. 64.

3. Abraham Rotstein "Leadership and Bondage in Luther and Marx," *Journal of Political Philosophy*, 18, No. 1. The quote that follows from Hegel is on p. 75.

4. Robert C. Tucker, ed., "Contribution to the Critique of Hegel's *Philosophy of Right*: Introduction," in *The Marx-Engels Reader*, 2nd ed., p. 60. Where possible, references to Marx's writings will be made to this very useful collection.

5. Quoted in Rotstein, "Leadership and Bondage," pp. 83 and 90. The quote that follows is on p. 75.

6. The quotes are from MECW, I, 636 and 638.

7. For details of this and what follows, cf. Fritz Raddatz, *Karl Marx: A Political Biography*, trans. Richard Berry (Boston: Little, Brown & Co., 1978 (original German 1975), especially Chapter I.

8. For these figures, see Heinz Monz, *Karl Marx, Grundlagen der Entwicklung zu Leben und Werk* (Trier: Nco-Verlag, 1973). Monz is the best source for information on Trier, but unfortunately no English translation yet exists. According to Monz, the total population of Trier in 1825 was 12,686, of whom 11,927 were Catholic, 500 Evangelical, and 259 Jewish. The population grew to 14,862 in 1835, with 13,816 Catholic, 782 Evangelical, and 264 Jewish (p. 58).

9. David McLellan, ed., *Karl Marx: Interviews and Recollections* (Totowa; New Jersey: Barnes and Noble Books, 1981), p. 53.

10. See MECW, Vol. I. The quotes that follow are from this edition.

11. MECW, I, 337, In this case, I have used the translation in *Writings of the Young Marx on Philosophy and Society*, Loyd D. Easton and Kurt H. Guddat ed. and trans., by Karl Marx (Garden City, New York: Doubleday & Co., 1967), p. 144.

12. Tucker, *Reader*, p. 595.

13. Isaiah Berlin, "Benjamin Disraeli, Karl Marx and the Search for Identity," in *Against the Current* (New York: Penguin Books, 1982), offers a wise and empathic discussion of possible "Jewish self-hatred" in Marx, placing it in the context of the marginality experienced by many Jews in the early 19th century, as they emerged from the ghettos into the mainstream of Western society.

IV. FATHER AND SON, AND THE GHOST OF HEGEL

1. MECW, I, 643.

2. The letter is given in full in MECW, I, 10–21.

3. Heinrich Marx's letters to Karl are to be found in MECW, Vol. I.

4. These statements are in MECW, I, 661, 681, and 672.

5. The concept of a double bind has been elaborated by Gregory Bateson, to describe a situation, for example, where a mother conveys a mixed message to a child, such as asking the child to kiss her but then averting her cheek. Bateson saw such frustration as a frequent part of the etiology of schizophrenia. For an account of Bateson's theory, see David Lipset, *Gregory Bateson, the Legacy of a Scientist* (Englewood Cliffs, New Jersey: Prentice-Hall Inc., 1980), especially pp. 206–19. I am using the concept in a very general, non-clinical sense.

6. MECW, I, 670–674.

7. MECW, p. 670.

V. PROMETHEAN REVOLUTIONARY, OR DICTATOR?

1. This statement is reported by Erik H. Erikson, *Childhood and Society* (New York: W. W. Norton & Co., 1963), pp. 264–65, and repeated in his *Identity, Youth and Crisis* (New York: W. W. Norton & Co., 1968), p. 136. Erikson never identifies the original questioner to whom Freud was responding, but only says that the questioner was asking Freud what he thought a normal person should be able to do well.

2. Marx to Jenny Marx, 15 December 1863, MECW, XXX, 643.

3. Marx to Jenny Marx, 21 June 1856, MEW, XXIX, 535.

4. Marx to Engels, 31 July, 1851, MEW, XXVII, 293.

5. For a full and sympathetic account, see Yvonne Karp, *Eleanor Marx* (New York: Pantheon Books, 1972), I, 289–97.

6. MECW, I, 28. The surviving version of the Dissertation itself follows this dedication. Marx's "Notebooks on Epicurean Philosophy" are on pp. 405–509.

7. MECW, I, 85. Also, Tucker, *Reader*, 10.

8. MECW, I, 491.

9. For another approach to the Promethean theme, cf. Kolakowski, *Main Currents*, I, 412–14.

10. The drawing can be found in Blumenberg, *Portrait*, p. 47.

11. Marx to Arnold Ruge, 25 January 1843, in MECW, I, 397–98.

12. Bruce Mazlish, *The Revolutionary Ascetic* (New York: Basic Books, 1976).

13. McLellan, *Interviews*, p. xv.

14. J. L. Talmon, *The Origins of Totalitarian Democracy* (New York: Praeger, 1960), pp. 2 and 11.

15. Richard N. Hunt, *The Political Ideas of Marx and Engels* (Pittsburgh: University of Pittsburgh Press, 1974), p. 339. The quote that follows is on p. xiii. A most incisive treatment of the general subject under consideration here is Stanley Moore, *Three Tactics: The Background in Marx* (New York: Monthly Review Press, 1963).

16. Hunt, *Political Ideas*, p. 13.
17. Hunt, *Political Ideas*, p. 342.
18. MECW I, 183 and 220–21. I use the translations in *Writings of the Young Marx on Philosophy and Society*, trans. and ed. Loyd D. Easton and Kurt H. Guddat, pp. 108 and 134–35.
19. Tucker, *Reader*, p. 22.
20. McLellan, *Interviews*, pp. 12 and 15.
21. Quoted in Mazlish, *Ascetic*, p. 40.
22. Tucker, *Reader*, p. 595.

VI. MARX WITH A HUMAN FACE

1. Tucker, *Reader*, p. 28. All quotes that follow are from this edition, and can easily be found there; hence, I give no further specific page references.
2. As Marx wrote Arnold Ruge, 13 March 1843: "I have just been visited by the chief of the Jewish community here [Cologne], who has asked me for a petition for the Jews to the Provincial Assembly, and I am willing to do it. However much I dislike the Jewish faith, Bauer's view seems to me too abstract" MECW, I, 400).
3. See, for example, Carr, *Study in Fanaticism*, especially p. 227.
4. Tucker, *Reader*, p. 53. All quotes following are from this edition, and can easily be found there.
5. Georges Sorel seized on exactly this point in his *Reflections on Violence* (trans. T. E. Hulme and J. Roth [New York: Collier Books, 1961] original French ed. 1906). "This doctrine [Marxist socialism] will evidently be inapplicable if the middle class and the proletariat do not oppose each other implacably with all the forces at their disposal; the more ardently capitalist the middle class is, the more the proletariat is full of warlike spirit and confident of its revolutionary strength, the more certain will be the success of the proletarian movement." As Sorel continues, "If, on the contrary, the middle class, led astray by the *chatter* of the preachers of ethics and sociology, return to an *ideal of conservative mediocrity*, seek to correct the *abuses* of economics, and wish to break with the barbarism of their predecessors, then one part of the forces which were to further the development of capitalism is employed in hindering it, an arbitrary and irrational element is introduced, and the future of the world becomes completely indeterminate" (pp. 88–89 and 89–90).
6. See Notes 13 and 16, Chapter I, pp. 161–162.
7. Tucker, *Reader*, p. 67. All quotes following are from this edition, and can easily be found there.
8. See, however, my book, *The Riddle of History* (New York: Harper & Row, 1966), Chapters VII and VIII, for Marx's relations to Comte.
9. Quoted in Sidney Hook, *From Hegel to Marx: Studies in the Intellectual*

Development of Karl Marx (1950; rpt. Ann Arbor: The University of Michigan Press, 1962), p. 224. This is an excellent treatment. For another account, see David McLellan, *The Young Hegelians and Karl Marx* (London: Macmillan & Co., 1969).

10. For this quote from Adam Smith and the one following, see *The Wealth of Nations*, any edition, Book I, Chapter VIII.

VII. THE MATERIALIST INTERPRETATION OF HISTORY

1. The text can be found conveniently in Tucker, *Reader*, pp. 143–45.
2. The most important part of *The German Ideology*, Part I, is in Tucker, *Reader*, pp. 147–200. The complete text is in MECW, Vol. V. As a single, whole volume the full translation into English can be found in an edition published in Moscow by Progress Publishers, 1964. The quotes I use are all from Part I, and can be found readily in Tucker, *Reader*.
3. William Godwin, *Enquiry Concerning Human Justice*, 3rd ed., 2 vols. (London: 1978), II, 528 and 527.
4. *Harmonian Man: Selected Writings of Charles Fourier*, ed. Mark Poster (Garden City, New York: Doubleday & Co., 1971), p. 13. For a complete enumeration of Marx's readings, see Maximilien Rubel and Margaret Manale, *Marx Without Myth: A Chronological Study of His Life and Work* (New York: Harper & Row, 1975). Along with the list of readings, the authors give a useful and extended summary of Marx's life and the contents of his writings, as well as a chronological account of contemporary events. Marx had also written in *The Holy Family* that "Fourier's assertion that the right to fish, to hunt, etc., are inborn rights of men is one of genius" MECW, IV, p. 88).
5. W. H. Oliver, "Owen in 1817: The Millennialist Moment," in *Robert Owen: Prophet of the Poor*, ed. Sidney Pollard and John Salt (London: Macmillan & Co., 1971), p. 166.
6. Quoted in Lewis S. Feuer, *Marx and the Intellectuals* (Garden City, New York: Doubleday & Co., 1969), p. 166. Feuer's essay, "The Alienated Americans and Their Influence on Marx and Engels," from which this quote is taken, is an interesting treatment of its subject.
7. Though Marx would argue otherwise, there is a tension in his claim to both scientific certainty and to freely willed action. Kolakowski expresses Marx's claim well:

> Marx's emphasis on the self-awareness of the proletariat in the process of emancipation is important in connection with the objection, sometimes put forward at a later date, that he appeared to believe that the revolution would come about as the result of an impersonal historical force, irrespective of the free activity of man. From his point of view there is no dilemma as between historical necessity and conscious ac-

tion, since the class-consciousness of the proletariat is not only a condition of the revolution but is itself the historical process in which the revolution comes to maturity. (*Main Currents*, p. 148).

Like Hegel, according to Kolakowski, Marx saw world history as determined by reason, and thus open to man's comprehension. Even "unreasonable" elements—war, capitalism—served a reasonable purpose, i.e., the dialectical progression to a perfect, unalienated existence. According to Marx, in earlier times, i.e., before, say, Hegel, man was ruled by an objective historical process; now, in Marx's time, man can become conscious of that process and take control of his own future (cf. Iring Fetscher, "The Relationship of Marxism to Hegel," *Marx and Marxism* (New York: Herder & Herder, 1971). This conscious understanding—in Hegel's case idealistic, in Marx's materialistic—can be seen as the equivalent of scientific understanding of the historical world, the counterpart to Darwin's theory of evolution in the natural world. Once the proletariat has the correct consciousness, Marx believed, it can and will then play its revolutionary role freely. In this interpretation of Marx's views, he merely shows the objective possibility of a revolutionary process—the conditions not under man's control but given to him—wherein the proletariat can destroy the old and construct a new society. Marx is not, like a natural scientist, presenting us with deterministic laws, which must necessarily produce a certain outcome, independent of man's voluntaristic actions.

As just stated Marx's ideas penetrate deep into the question of how a social science is possible—the "what is–what should be" problem—and are very attractive. Such plausibility, however, I would argue, is undercut by Marx's chiliastic, revolutionary desires, which require a communist revolution, not just as a possibility, but as a certainty. Marx's wish—his will—overcame his effort at science, which instead of being a true science, limited and open to empirical qualification, was a Hegelian one, basically metaphysical in spite of its materialistic dress. In this sense, the humanist Marx weakens or destroys the possibility of a truly scientific Marx. The result is Marxism, a secular religion in scientific guise, whose millennial aspirations can readily lead to undesirable, totalistic ends, which cannot be averted easily as some Marxist scholars would like by an appeal to a young, humanist Marx. Marx's humanism and his science, in the end, turn out to be all of one piece.

8. Again, an easily accessible version can be found in Tucker, *Reader*.

9. See, for example, Patrick H. Hutton, *The Cult of the Revolutionary Tradition: The Blanquists in French Politics, 1864–1893* (Berkeley: University of California Press, 1981). For secret societies in general, and similar developments, see James H. Billington's wide-ranging book, *Fire in the Minds of Men: Origins of the Revolutionary Faith* (New York: Basic Books, 1980).

10. Engels to Marx, 23/24 November 1847, MEW, XXVII, 107, quoted in

McLellan, *Interviews*, p. 179. The classic edition of the *Manifesto* is that of D. Ryazanoff (London: M. Lawrence, 1930).

11. Tucker, *Reader*, p. 472.

12. Carlyle, for example, uses these phrases at a number of places in his *Past and Present*. See, for example, Thomas Carlyle, *Sartor Resartus: Heroes, Past and Present* (London: Chapman & Hill, MCMX), pp. 29, 58, 126, 146, and 160.

13. For Marx's role in the First International, especially in regard to Britain, see H. Collins and C. Abramsky, *Karl Marx and the British Labor Movement: Years of the First International* (London: Macmillan & Co., 1965).

14. Marx to Adolf Cluss, 15 September 1853, MEW, XXVII, 592. (In one of his rare errors, McLellan cites this letter as written in October; see McLellan, *Interviews*, p. 285). The letter can also be found in MECW, XXXIX, 366–67.

VIII. THE MYSTERY OF CAPITAL

1. The first quote is from Robert Paul Wolff, "How To Read *Das Kapital*," *The Massachusetts Review*, 21, No. 4 (Winter 1980), p. 765, the second from Wolff's "Piero Sraffa and the Rehabilitation of Classical Political Economy," *Social Research*, 49, No. 1 (Spring 1982), p. 213. See, also, his "A Critique and Reinterpretation of Marx's Labor Theory of Value," *Philosophy and Public Affairs*, 10, No. 2 (Spring 1981). The effort to rehabilitate Marx as an economist is being pursued, for example, by the economist, Samuel Bowles at the University of Massachusetts, Amherst and Mark Wartofsky, a philosopher at Boston University. Earlier, Joan Robinson, *An Essay on Marxian Economics*, 2nd ed. (London: Macmillan, 1966) began Marx's rehabilitation as a major economic theorist. Along these same lines, while some scholars, as we have seen, now emphasize the early writings of Marx in order to defend him, others counterattack on a different front by emphasizing anew the later writings, which include the economic works per se. Thus, David McLellan in his excellent collection, *Karl Marx: Selected Writings* (Oxford: Oxford University Press, 1977), states, "Over recent years increasing attention has been paid to the three works that Marx produced between 1857 and 1867—the *Grundrisse*, the *Theories of Surplus Value*, and *Capital*. On almost any reading of Marx these constituted his main theoretical contribution . . . [and] constitute the centrepiece of Marx's work" (p. 1). Even McLellan admits, however, that "many of the positions taken up by Marx in 1844 were still present in the *Grundrisse* and even in *Capital* (p. 75)." As is obvious, I, too, am arguing for a unified Marx, but for one whose major theoretical contribution is already in place by the middle of the 19th century and whose meaning we can readily discern by that time.

2. A magisterial treatment of these developments, and, indeed, of the whole

development of economic thought is to be found in Joseph Schumpeter, *History of Economic Analysis* (New York: Oxford University Press, 1954).

3. There are many editions in English of the first volume of *Capital*, (hereafter referred to as *Capital*). As yet, the volume containing it has not appeared in the MECW. Eden Paul and Cedar Paul have made a translation from the 4th German edition, published in 1890, revised by Engels (London: J.M. Dent & Sons, 1951). Samuel Moore and Edward Aveling made a translation from the 3rd German edition, also revised by Engels, and it is this translation that is reprinted, in a substantial but by no means full, version in Tucker, *Reader*. The part immediately under consideration here, on capitalist accumulation, comes at the end of the book. The quote can be found in Tucker, *Reader*, p. 437.

4. Thomas Carlyle, *Past and Present*, Book I, Chapter I, any edition. Engels, incidentally, reviewed Carlyle's book for the *Deutsch-Französische Jahrbücher*.

5. Tucker, *Reader*, p. 343. (I have used, however, the Paul translation, I, 164; the differences are slight.)

6. See Schumpeter, *Economic Analysis*, p. 556.

7. E. P. Thompson, *The Making of the English Working Class* (1963; rpt. New York: Vintage Books, 1966).

8. John Foster, *Class Struggle and the Industrial Revolution: Early Industrial Capitalism in Three English Towns* (New York: St. Martin's Press, 1974).

9. John Foster, "Nineteenth-Century Towns—A Class Dimension," in *The Study of Urban History*, ed. H. J. Dyos (New York: St. Martin's Press, 1968), p. 289.

IX. THE IMPORTANCE OF BEING KARL MARX

1. Albert Schweitzer, *The Psychiatric Study of Jesus*, trans. Winfred Overholser (Boston: Beacon Press, 1948).

2. Richard Lebeaux, *Young Man Thoreau* (Amherst: University of Massachusetts Press, 1975).

3. A convenient edition is Henry David Thoreau, *Walden; or Life in the Woods* (1854; rpt. New York: Rinehart & Co., 1957). The quotes given are on pp. 3, 4, 29, and 37. The quotes that follow are on pp. 1, 6, 52, and 58.

4. Lebeaux, *Thoreau*, p. 215.

5. Thoreau, *Walden*, p. 321.

6. Quoted in Lebeaux, *Thoreau*, p. 245.

7. Thoreau, *Walden*, p. 321.

8. Quoted in Lebeaux, *Thoreau*, p. 65.

9. Hutton, *Revolutionary Tradition*, p. 22.

10. As with Marx, books on Einstein either gloss over or misrepresent his personal relations; great men are not supposed to exhibit less than praiseworthy

human qualities. Abraham Pais, in his solid, scientific biography, *Subtle is the Lord: The Science and the Life of Albert Einstein* (Oxford: Clarendon Press, 1982), glosses over the matter by saying, "These contacts [with Einstein's children] were not always easy, since Mileva [Einstein's first wife] never reconciled herself to the separation and subsequent divorce" (p. 241). Cf. p. 301.

11. Tucker, *Reader*, p. 296.

12. As this is an important point, the interested reader might want to consult, for example, J. H. Hexter, "The Myth of the Middle Class in Tudor England" in *Reappraisals in History* (Northwestern University Press, 1961). As another example, I cite the lengthy statement by Elie Kedourie, reviewing a book on modern Iran, by an otherwise excellent scholar, Ervand Abrahamian.

Whether his approach is "neo-Marxist" or plain Marxist, Abrahamian cannot avoid operating with the notion of class. The Marxist notion of class and class-relations, in so far as it is intelligible, is logically tied to that of the ownership (or nonownership) of the means of production. In the Marxist schema a middle class, a bourgeoisie, is the necessary concomitant of capitalism. The middle class is middle because it follows, is indeed conjured up by, the workings of feudalism. As the engine of historical change, it is in turn supplanted by the industrial working class to which "capitalism" willy-nilly gives birth. This account of social and economic change derives its plausibility from its implicit reference to Western European history, where a mercantile and professional bourgeoisie gradually asserted itself and challenged a landed nobility. But how is one to make use of the idea of a middle class in the Middle East, or India, or China—let alone set it up as the motor and mainspring of social and political change?

Consider the difficulties in which Abrahamian gets entangled by his attempt to discern a Persian middle class, and to specify its political role. He first identifies a "traditional middle class": it has ties to the traditional economy and "the traditional Shi'i ideology," and is said to have become aware of itself as a class, conscious of its grievances, when Western economic penetration threatened its commercial interests. But there are two other middle classes. One is a "comprador bourgeoisie" created outside the bazaar by the introduction of European capital and by the capitulations granted to European business men; the other is a "salaried middle class." The latter comprises the intelligentsia and those trained for a profession, who have been affected by Western ideas. They are *munavver alfekr, rushanfekr* (enlightened thinkers), *kravatis* (tie-wearers), *dawlatis* (government officials). In the nineteenth century these groups, the author says, formed "a mere stratum"; but during Reza Shah's reign they were transformed into "a social class with similar relationships to the mode of production, the means of administration, and the process of modernization."

Class, as against a mere stratum, is not lightly to be invoked in a Marxist or even a neo-Marxist scheme. A class not only has a relationship to the mode of production, but this relationship determines its political stance, and its position in the class-struggle. Here, however, we have not just one middle class but three. What are the relationships between these three middle classes? Do they struggle against one another, against the class they are supplanting, and against the class which will inevitably supplant them?

Since there is a class waiting to supplant them (as is of course self-evident, according to class-analysis), and since it is (of necessity) the working class, its interests must (precisely because it is a class) find political expression. The Tudeh Party is (must be) the voice, the emanation of the working class of Iran. The party was the champion of "workers, peasants, intellectuals, traders, and craftsmen." It is claimed to be the "vanguard of the proletariat and landless peasantry." But if we look more closely at the Party what do we find? We find, as Abrahamian tells us, that "it was the modern middle class that formed the major portion of the party's top, middle, and lower echelons. The modern middle class", he goes on to say, "also made up an important portion of the party's general rank and file and sympathizers." We are also told that—*mirabile dictu*—rapid modernization and industrialization, which drew some 4,000,000 peasants into the cities, tended not to strengthen, but actually to weaken the Tudeh!

If we cling, then, to class-analysis we find ourselves in a topsy-turvy world (*Times Literary Supplement*, December 3, 1982, p. 1327).

13. Friedrich Nietzsche, *Beyond Good and Evil*, translated by Marianne Cowan (Chicago: Henry Regnery Co., 1955), 6.
14. Sigmund Freud, *New Introductory Lectures on Psychoanalysis* (1933 [1932]), Chapter XXV, "The Question of a *Weltanschauung*," in *The Standard Edition of the Complete Psychological Works of Sigmund Freud*, 24 vols., James Strachey (London: The Hogarth Press 1964), XXII, 178 and 180.
15. MECW, I, 684.
16. Thomas Robert Malthus, *Population: The First Essay* (Ann Arbor: The University of Michigan Press, 1959), p. 62.
17. Tucker, *Reader*, p. 24.

X. A CONCLUSION WITHOUT AN END

1. Adam Smith, *Lectures on Jurisprudence*, ed. R. L. Meek, D. D. Raphael and P. G. Stein (Indianapolis: Liberty Classics [reprinted from The Glasgow Edition of the Works and Correspondence of Adam Smith], 1982), pp. 338 and 404.

2. Gaetano Mosca, *The Ruling Class*, trans. Hannah D. Kahn; rpt. New York: McGraw-Hill, 1939 [original 1896 and 1923]). Robert Michels, *Political Parties*, trans. Eden Paul and Cedar Paul (Glencoe, Illinois, The Free Press, 1949 [original German 1911]).
3. Hugh Trevor-Roper, "The Historical Spirit," *Times Literary Supplement*, October 8, 1982, p. 1088. This is a good short treatment of the subject, which, in part, I am paraphrasing.
4. Walter L. Adamson, "Marx's Four Histories: An Approach to his Intellectual Development," *History & Theory*, Beiheft XX, 20, No. 4, 1981.
5. Adamson, "Four Histories," p. 399.
6. Marx to Engels, 20 February 1866, MEW, XXX, 183. (I have used the translation in Jerrold Seigel, *Marx's Fate: The Shape of a Life* (Princeton: Princeton University Press, 1978), p. 329.)

EPILOGUE

1. For an indication of one direction in which such a critique could be carried, see Neva R. Goodwin and Bruce Mazlish "The Wealth of Adam Smith," *Harvard Business Review*, July–August 1983, pp. 52–65.
2. Quoted in Edgar Snow, *The Long Revolution* (New York: Random House, 1972), p. 242.
3. Erik H. Erikson, *Insight and Responsibility* (New York: W. W. Norton & Co., 1964), p. 242.

Bibliography

Of the making of books on Karl Marx there is no end. Every year dozens of books and hundreds of articles appear, in all languages. What follows is, needless to say, a drastic selection, limited, with a few exceptions, to works in English. Happily, almost all the books listed also have bibliographies, and the interested reader will be carried further and further into the literature by a kind of chain reaction.

Works

There are two major German language editions of Marx's and Engels's works and correspondence:

Karl Marx and Friedrich Engels. *Werke*. East Berlin: The Institute for Marxism-Leninism, 1956ff. Referred to as MEW.

Karl Marx and Friedrich Engels. *Historisch-Kritische Gesamtausgabe: Werke/Schriften/Briefe*. Ed. D. Rjazanov. Frankfurt-Berlin, 1927ff.

In English, there is the ongoing publication, *Karl Marx and Frederick Engels: Collected Works*. New York: International Publishers (jointly with Lawrence and Wishart, London, and Progress Publishers, Moscow), 1975—. Vol. 40 had already appeared at the time of this writing, out of a planned total of 50. Referred to as MECW.

Biographies

Berlin, Isaiah. *Karl Marx, His Life and Work*. London: Oxford University Press, 1939, and numerous reissues. A standard, short treatment, which, as expected from its author, is sane, scholarly, and readable. Now, naturally, somewhat outdated.

Blumenberg, Werner. *Portrait of Marx*. Trans. Douglas Scott. New York: Herder and Herder, 1972 (original German 1962). A short, pungent biography, with excellent illustrations. The author's sympathies for his subject occasionally cause him to be naïve.

Carr, E. H. *Karl Marx, A Study in Fanaticism*. London: J.M. Dent and Sons, 1934. Written with passion and great insight; very lively. The subtitle suggests the author's critical attitude to his subject. One of the best studies, though necessarily somewhat outdated by the appearance of new materials since its publication, in terms of facts if not judgments.

Cornu, Auguste. *Karl Marx et Friedrich Engels, leur vie et leur oeuvre*. 4 Vols. Vol. I, *Les annés d'enfance et de jeunesse, la gauche hegélienne, 1818/1820–1844*. Paris: Presses Universitaires de France, 1955. For those who read French, a fundamental treatment of the early years. Three other volumes continue the story.

McLellan, David. *Karl Marx: His Life and Thought*. New York: Harper and Row, 1973. One of the best, taking into account new materials on Marx's life. Though the author is favorable to his subject, he writes in a very neutral and thorough fashion. Has a good bibliography. The same author's *Marx Before Marxism* (New York: Harper and Row, 1970) is a short version of Marx's life and work up to about 1844.

Mehring, Franz. *Karl Marx: The Story of His Life*. Trans. Edward Fitzgerald. Rpt. 1935; Ann Arbor: University of Michigan Press, 1962 (original German 1918). A classic biography, seriously out of date and highly uncritical. Very short on Marx's early life.

Nicolaievsky, Boris, and Otto Maenchen-Helfen. *Karl Marx: Man and Fighter*. Trans. Gwenda David and Eric Mosbacher. London, 1936 and rev. ed, 1973. Emphasizes Marx's political activities.

Raddatz, Fritz J. *Karl Marx: A Political Biography*. Trans. Richard Barry. Boston: Little, Brown and Co., 1978 (original German 1975). One of the best, although occasionally too cantankerous, and very up-to-date in its coverage; the author treats his subject without illusion, and perhaps even hostilely. Has a good bibliography.

Rubel, Maximilien, and Margaret Manale. *Marx Without Myth: A Chronological Study of His Life and Work*. New York: Harper and Row, 1976. The authors are knights in armor, defending Marx against any charges that his ideas could possibly lead to Stalinism, but this does not prevent them from giving a sound, scholarly account—Rubel is an outstanding Marxist scholar—in chronological order, of Marx's life and work. Extremely useful.

NOTE Among efforts to look at Marx's life and work in overtly psychological terms are: Arnold Künzli, *Karl Marx, Eine Psychographie* (Wien, Austria:

Europe Verlag, 1966), written from a Jungian standpoint. A long work, it has, unfortunately, not been translated into English; see, however, the review-essay by Herbert Moller, in *History and Theory*, VIII, 3 (1969). Otto Rühle, *Karl Marx* (London: George Allen and Unwin, 1929) is an early and rather crude attempt at a psychological study. Jerrold Seigel, *Marx's Fate* (Princeton: Princeton University Press, 1978) is a psychologically astute, scholarly study, which, making few concessions in its prose to the average reader, seeks to understand the "inner unity" of Marx's life. It also has a useful bibliography and footnotes.

Commentaries

Acton, H.B. *The Illusion of the Epoch: Marxism-Leninism as a Philosophical Creed*. London: Cohen and West, 1955. A critical treatment of the philosophical assumptions of Marxism-Leninism.

Althusser, Louis. *For Marx*. Trans. Ben Brewster. London: The Penguin Press, 1969 (original 1966). A badly written piece of Marxist apologetics, which, nevertheless, has made quite a stir. Argues for a radical break between a young and old Marx, around 1845, and prefers the later, scientific to the humanistic, philosophical Marx. One gets the flavor of Althusser's views in his remark that "Marx's discovery is a scientific discovery without historical precedent, in its nature and effects" (p. 13).

Avineri, Shlomo. *The Social and Political Thought of Karl Marx*. Cambridge: Cambridge University Press, 1968. Argues against the thesis that a gap existed between the "young" and "old" Marx. The author examines Marx's intellectual origins and emphasizes Marx's indebtedness to Hegel.

Buber, M.M. *Karl Marx's Interpretation of History*. 2nd edition. New York, 1965 (1st ed. 1927). An early discussion of historical materialism.

Fetscher, Iring. *Marx and Marxism*. New York: Herder and Herder, 1971. The work of an intelligent Marxist who wishes to dissociate Marx's critical thought from dogmatic Soviet Marxism. Fetscher does so by examining the young and old Marx, the relationship of Marx to Hegel, and alienation. He sees an inherent unity in Marx's writings. While he gets too absorbed in internal Marxist polemics, Fetscher does offer a useful introduction to the "Socialism with a Human Face" debates.

Hook, Sidney. *From Hegel to Marx: Studies in the Intellectual Development of Karl Marx*. 2nd ed. Ann Arbor: University of Michigan Press, 1962 (1st ed. 1950). Still a useful study of Marx's relations to Hegel and the Young Hegelians. Also see his *Towards the Understanding of Karl Marx* (New York, 1933), a pro-Marx book whose views the author would repudiate today.

Hunt, Richard. *The Political Ideas of Marx and Engels*. Vol. I. Pittsburgh: University of Pittsburgh Press, 1975. An effort, sympathetic but fair-minded, to show that Marx favored what we would today call participatory democracy rather than totalitarianism. The various pieces of evidence are presented in a scholarly rather than polemical fashion.

Jordan, Z.A. *The Evolution of Dialectical Materialism: A Philosophical and Sociological Analysis.* New York: St. Martin's Press, 1967. An exhaustive study, arguing that Marx was a naturalist thinker, applying his ideas to history and society, rather than a dialectical materialist. Engels alone, according to Jordan, was the author of dialectical materialism.

Kamenka, Eugene. *The Ethical Foundations of Marxism.* 2nd ed. London: Routledge and Kegan, 1972 (1st ed. 1962). A thorough philosophical study of the subject, which examines Marx's concepts of freedom and alienation as central to his work. Emphasizes the continuity of Marx's thought. While basically critical, it is also sympathetic and aims to understand Marx's intentions.

Kolakowski, Leszek. *Main Current of Marxism, Its Rise, Growth and Dissolution.* 3 volumes. Oxford: Clarendon Press, 1978. Volume 3 is concerned with "The Founders," and is a magisterial treatment of Marx and Engels's ideas and the philosophical context in which they originated. Chapter I, on "The Origins of Dialectic," traces it from antiquity through to Hegel, and is especially valuable for an understanding of the eschatological background to Marx's thinking. (Volumes II and III deal with Marxism, after Marx, as a doctrine.)

Lichtheim, George. *Marxism, an Historical and Critical Study.* New York: Frederick A. Praeger, 1961. This is a useful study of Marxist theory from its origins as well as an account of the Marxist movement up until 1948.

Lukacs, Georg. *History and Class Consciousness.* Trans. Rodney Livingstone. Cambridge, MA: The MIT Press, 1971 (original German edition, 1923). Reasserts the importance of Hegel's influence on Marx. This book has played a major role in the debates over the young and old Marx and their connection. Though a believing and even subservient Marxist, who fell over himself apologizing for his work, Lukacs broached some seminal ideas within the Leninist orthodoxy.

Lunn, Eugene. *Marxism and Modernism: An Historical Study of Lukacs, Brecht, Benjamin and Adorno.* Berkeley: University of California Press, 1982. While, as its subtitle suggests, not per se a study of Marx and aesthetics, it does offer a useful introduction to the subject and includes a fine bibliography on works relating to Marx, Marxism, and Marxist Aesthetics.

Marcuse, Herbert. *Reason and Revolution: Hegel and the Rise of Social Theory.* London: Oxford University Press, 1941. While mainly devoted to an analysis of Hegel, useful in showing the background against which Marx sought to follow up on Hegel's effort to move from philosophy to social theory.

Moore, Stanley. *Three Tactics: The Background in Marx.* New York: Monthly Review Press, 1963. Analyzes Marx's relation to later Marxism by setting up three alternative models in his thinking as to how the transition to communism was to take place: the pattern of permanent revolution, of increasing misery, and of competing systems, i.e. three different tactics. A clear, succinct presentation, to be read in conjunction with Hunt, *Political Ideas*.

Ollman, Bertell. *Alienation: Marx's Conception of Man in Capitalist Society*. Cambridge: Cambridge University Press, 1971. Approaches its subject through an interesting analysis of Marx's language and his conception of human nature. "Theological" in approach, in the sense that the author stays entirely within Marx's writings, with no glance at the real world. While trying to strike a critical stance, the author admits to his Marxist sympathies—and is basically uncritical. The style of writing makes for heavy going.

Robinson, Joan. *An Essay on Marxian Economics*. 2d ed. London: Macmillan, 1966 (1st ed. 1942). A reexamination of Marx's economic doctrines and an attempt to make them relevant to the contemporary scene. May be compared to Paul M. Sweezy, *The Theory of Capital Development* (New York: Monthly Review, 1956). Robinson's is a short, dry, technical book for economists, which nevertheless vibrates with feeling. Sympathetic to Marxist ideals, the author impartially examines Marx's economic doctrines—especially as found in Vols. II and III of *Capital*—in the light of current, i.e., 1940s, economic analysis. For the 2nd edition, Robinson concludes, "The world picture has slipped out of the frame of Marx's argument. But the questions that he posed are still relevant today, while the academics continue to erect elegant elaborations on trivial topics" (XV). Her most critical comments are reserved for Marx's theory of value, which she considers an unnecessary metaphysical concept, and whose place is more adequately taken by price.

Tucker, Robert C. *Philosophy and Myth in Karl Marx*. Cambridge: Cambridge University Press, 1961. An important and penetrating study of Marx's early writings and also of *Capital*. Argues against the view that there is a gulf between a young and old Marx, while emphasizing the eschatological theme in Marx's work. I find Tucker's arguments compatible.

Wilson, Edmund. *To the Finland Station*. Garden City, New York: Doubleday and Co. 1940. A highly readable, brilliant account of Marx's predecessors, starting with Vico, and successors, ending with Lenin. A literary masterpiece.

Index of Subjects

Index of Names